MAN'S QUEST FOR SECURITY

BF
575
.S35
F3
1970

Man's Quest for Security

A Symposium

Sidney Hook · Kingsley Davis
Howard P. Rome, M.D. · Harold W. Stoke · Henry S. Beers
Charls E. Walker · General Thomas Power, USAF (Ret.)

Edited by Edwin J. Faulkner

Essay Index Reprint Series

 BOOKS FOR LIBRARIES PRESS
FREEPORT, NEW YORK

Copyright © 1966 by the University of Nebraska Press
All rights reserved

Reprinted 1970 by arrangement

INTERNATIONAL STANDARD BOOK NUMBER:
0-8369-1921-1

LIBRARY OF CONGRESS CATALOG CARD NUMBER:
74-117790

PRINTED IN THE UNITED STATES OF AMERICA

Foreword

Man's quest for security is eternal. In prehistoric times it was elemental and constant, concerned with physical protection against the forces of nature. As civilization has advanced, this quest has become more sophisticated, involving a myriad of social, economic, and political devices. Since security in its broadest sense is a universal aspiration of mankind, interest in it is widespread, engaging the thought and testing the ingenuity of the scholar and the urchin in the street, the professional person and the layman, the informed and the ignorant. Security and man's never ending quest for it have many dimensions. A comprehensive examination of them requires analysis from the viewpoints of widely differing disciplines.

The year 1965 marked the seventy-fifth anniversary of Woodmen Accident and Life Company of Lincoln, Nebraska. Desiring to make what would be a significant contribution to constructive thinking about human security, the Company was privileged to join with the University of Nebraska in sponsoring a symposium whose theme was "Man's Quest for Security." The symposium was held on the campus of the University, November 4–5, 1965.

The interest of the Company in the subject of security derives from the nature of its business—the provision of protection against the financial consequences of the three great hazards, death, disability, and dependent old age. Dr. William Haber, Dean of the College of Literature, Science, and Art, University of Michigan, noted in the first Clarence Axman Lecture that "All of life—and business activity is no exception—is surrounded with a substantial degree of insecurity. Every institution in our society whose object is to provide protection against insecurity, whether to corporate institutions or families and individuals, against the vicissitudes of change, against the uncertainties of tomorrow, performs an indisposable function in our society."

The theme of the symposium was developed by eminent scholars representing the fields of philosophy, sociology, medicine, political science, military science, insurance, and economics. Following each principal presentation, two discussants offered a brief commentary on it. The opinions expressed by the speakers and discussants were their own and do not necessarily represent the views of either the University of Nebraska or Woodmen Accident and Life Company. This volume consists of the papers and discussion presented at the symposium. It has been published because the sponsors believe that this material should be shared with as wide an audience as possible. The problems of security are every man's business.

Special thanks for the success of the symposium are due Dr. Davis W. Gregg, President of the American College of Life Underwriters, who suggested the theme and gave great encouragement to the sponsors, and to the faculty and staff of the University of Nebraska, particularly Dr. Adam C. Breckenridge, Vice Chancellor and Dean of the Faculties. Their individual interest and collective support made the symposium possible in an atmosphere of academic excellence.

> E. J. FAULKNER
> President
> Woodmen Accident and Life Company

Contents

A Philosopher's View: Sidney Hook	1
Comment by Charles H. Patterson	18
Comment by Robert H. Hurlbutt III	21
A Sociologist's View: Kingsley Davis	25
Comment by Alan P. Bates	49
Comment by the Reverend J. Ford Forsyth, Th.D.	53
A Psychiatrist's View: Howard P. Rome, M.D.	57
Comment by Robert J. Stein, M.D.	75
Comment by Merrill T. Eaton, M.D.	78
A Political Scientist's View: Harold W. Stoke	81
Comment by Jasper B. Shannon	100
Comment by W. Robert Parks	106
An Insurer's View: Henry S. Beers	109
Comment by Curtis M. Elliott	124
Comment by John C. Angle	129
An Economist's View: Charls E. Walker	133
Comment by Campbell R. McConnell	169
Comment by Walter S. Henrion	174
A Military Scientist's View: General Thomas S. Power, USAF (Ret.)	181

Introductory Remarks

by

DR. CLIFFORD M. HARDIN

Chancellor, University of Nebraska

It is a privilege to extend greetings on behalf of the University of Nebraska to all of you who are guests this week, and to say to you that we at the University are happy and proud to have been invited by Woodmen Accident and Life Company to join with them in this endeavor.

The value and potential of educational projects sponsored jointly by universities and institutions of the business and industrial worlds have long been recognized. Only infrequently, however, have such programs been conducted, and this is one of those unusual occasions. The excellence of this particular symposium program and the response demonstrated by your attendance promise success for the presentations and discussions which are to follow.

You are participating this week in a type of activity which seems destined to become an increasing part of the program of the modern university. I am certain that in line with the theme of the symposium, "Man's Quest for Security," people of all ages and all walks of life will find it desirable to return more frequently in the future to an educational situation either to sharpen their perspective or to become updated in their fields of special interest.

Along with other forms of life, man has struggled with the basic practical problems of getting food and shelter and ensuring the continuation of his species. Man alone, however, has also sought to unravel the mysteries of his environment and his place in it. He has been concerned with the *reason* for his being. As a result, he has forever explored for new knowledge; he has reviewed his findings; and from time to time he has readjusted his concepts. All of these efforts have been directed toward a final goal of winning a total security of the mind and spirit, as well as of the body.

As the quest has continued, the importance of order in the search has become clearly apparent. The process of trial and error has given way to more effective efforts involving planning, logic, and science. Gradually our modern educational structure has adjusted to the new demands, and the pace is accelerating.

In this present decade, college enrollments across the country are approximately doubling. Many of us in education—in your states as well as in this one—are struggling with the problem of how to live with the bigness and still keep a personal atmosphere on our campuses. At the same time we are trying to improve our research capabilities, our graduate colleges, and all of the other responsibilities that are part of the university today. The challenge we all face is how to come out of this period of rapid expansion and growth not only bigger institutions but better ones.

We welcome the interest and the help of institutions which ordinarily operate outside the specific realm of education. We are especially grateful to Woodmen Accident and Life Company. And we are pleased to join with all of you in congratulating this company on completing seventy-five successful years, as well as having a management whose character and vision led it to the sponsorship of this symposium as the major event of its seventy-fifth anniversary celebration.

Remarks

by

the Honorable CARL. T. CURTIS
United States Senator from the State of Nebraska,
at the Evening Session and Banquet,
November 4, 1965

Chairman Faulkner, Governor Morrison, Chancellor Hardin, General Power, ladies and gentlemen:

As I listened to the fine addresses today at the symposium on "Man's Quest for Security," I pondered how this quest applies to those of us who run for office. Then I recalled what one of my colleagues from the South said a while back. He said, "You know, I've run for office in a good many ways, and I've figured out what is the best way to run. It is unopposed."

I have been told that what we need down in Washington is a government that realizes that two and two make four. This puts me in mind of the experience of the head of a federal bureau who decided that what he needed was a bright young assistant. He received many applications, sorted them over, and eliminated all but three applicants, who were summoned for oral interviews. In the course of the interview with the first young man, the bureau chief asked, "Young man, what do you say two and two make?" He replied, "Four." So, the chief wrote in his dossier, "Not much imagination; inclined to be conservative; probably honest." Well, the next young man came in and in due course he was asked, "What do you say that two and two make?" The young man replied, "Seven." The bureaucrat wrote in his record, "Shows real prospects; may have leadership possibilities; a young man to watch." Finally, the third young fellow came in and eventually was asked, "Young man, what do you say two and two make?" Quick as a flash, he answered, "Nine." The interviewer wrote down, "A real comer; definitely has leadership possibilities, a man to watch; real ability." Now, you probably wonder to which one the bureaucrat gave the job. He didn't give it to any of them—he appointed his nephew.

I wish that I might adequately express my happiness at being present on this stimulating and significant occasion. With all of you, it was my privilege today to listen to the scholarly and provocative addresses of Dr. Hook, Dr. Davis, Dr. Stoke, and Mr. Beers, and the incisive comment that followed. This evening, I look forward to the message of one of America's truly distinguished military men, General Thomas Power, former Commander-in-Chief of the Strategic Air Command.

Like you, I am deeply indebted to two great institutions—the University of Nebraska and Woodmen Accident and Life Company—for making this symposium possible. Over the years, it has been a heart-warming experience for me to follow the growth and development, to observe the expanding sphere of service of these two institutions. Just ten years ago I was privileged to have a part in the dedication of the beautiful home office building of Woodmen Accident and Life Company. For more than thirty years, it has been my good fortune to know of the aspirations and opportunities of the University and to have joined with all good Nebraskans in helping them to be realized. Thus you will understand why, like you, I am especially happy that these institutions, to which we feel so close and for which we have such respect, are joined in sponsoring so worth-while an endeavor as a symposium whose theme is "Man's Quest for Security."

It is uniquely appropriate, I think, for the University and a fine private insurer to collaborate in encouraging serious and constructive thought on so insistent and many-sided a subject.

Increasingly, during the past three decades, too many among us have come to regard security as the responsibility of an ever bigger federal government. They forget, or perhaps they never realized, as did William Hazlitt, that "In even the common affairs of life, how little security have we when we trust our happiness in the hands of others." Americans, over the years, have enjoyed such happiness and security as no other people has ever known. And it is my belief that this has been the case because the founding fathers created in our land an environment in which individual enterprise and opportunity were fostered and encouraged and were safeguarded equally against the intolerant majorities and the coercive minorities. In this atmosphere private enterprise has thrived to produce unequaled material abundance. In the same vein, the American climate has nurtured the finest educational system in the world. It has been the backbone of a strong, aggressive, and free America. We have moved a very long way from the simple life that prevailed when the American design was conceived. Laissez-faire economy no longer is possible or desirable. The simple democracy of the town meeting has been made obsolete, for state and national issues at least, by our vast population and the complexity of our problems. The little red schoolhouse is completely inadequate in the face of a body of knowledge that has been doubling every fourteen years. Yet for all of this, our fundamental reliance for security and happiness on the integrity and enterprise of millions of educated people has not changed.

Today, the responsibilities in the public interest borne by educators and businessmen are enormous. Private enterprisers have not only the essential task of producing all the goods and services to meet the demands of the consumer, to provide employment for our growing millions of workers, and to pay the staggering load of taxes required to maintain local, state, and national government. But increasingly, they have the difficult and often misunderstood responsibility of preserving our private enterprise system against those who would impair or destroy it.

Educators are confronted with the unprecedented challenge, not only in the swelling tide of millions of youngsters who seek and deserve the opportunity to learn, but with problems of what and how best to teach. The growing concern of the federal government with education is probably an inevitable consequence of two factors: first, the world struggle to contain Communism which demands for our survival, leadership and excellence in every field of learning, not just the physical sciences but the humanities and the social sciences as well; and second, the fact that for thirty years the federal government has so pre-empted the sources of revenues that the state and local governments have too often been unwilling or unable to make an adequate investment in education. And yet if our Republic is to endure, such an investment must be made and education must come to be regarded not as a right but as a duty. The gravest danger of the growing federal interest in education is that when federal monies are spent, federal dictation and control will follow. No federal subsidy is worth the loss of academic freedom coupled with responsibility that has given strength, vitality, integrity, and creativity to our schools and colleges. It is this danger to which I hope our educators will be constantly alert.

I have attempted to suggest that the responsibilities of leadership as we quest for happiness and security fall heavily on the shoulders of businessmen and educators, two groups so well represented here tonight. It may seem out of character for a politician to admit it, but you are more important to the future of our country than we who are in public office. You, through your teaching, through your leadership, mold and create the public attitudes that determine the government's program. So again I say it is heart-warming and hopeful to observe this meaningful collaboration of educators and businessmen on a subject of the greatest public interest. I thank you.

MAN'S QUEST FOR SECURITY

A Philosopher's View

SIDNEY HOOK

A philosopher and educator of international renown, SIDNEY HOOK is professor of philosophy and head of the department at New York University's Graduate School of Arts and Sciences. He has three times held Guggenheim Fellowships for research in European philosophy (1928, 1929, 1953) and in 1958 received a Ford Foundation Fellowship for the study of Asian philosophy and culture. In 1961–1962 Professor Hook was a Fellow at The Center for Advanced Study in the Behavioral Sciences at Stanford University. Among his recent books are *The Quest for Being* (1961), *From Hegel to Marx* (1962), and *Education for Modern Man* (1963). Professor Hook served as president of the American Philosophical Association (Eastern Division) in 1961–1962. He is a Fellow of the American Academy of Arts and Sciences.

CHARLES H. PATTERSON is a professor of philosophy, formerly chairman of the department, at the University of Nebraska; he is the author of *Philosophy of the Old Testament* (1953) and *Moral Standards* (1957). ROBERT H. HURLBUTT III, who also teaches philosophy at Nebraska, is the author of *Hume, Newton, and the Design Argument* (1965).

Man's quest for security has meant different things in different ages and different things to different persons in the same age. To discuss, therefore, the quest for security in the large, subjects one to the risk of appearing irrelevant to those who define the quest for security in terms of the gratification of immediately pressing social and economic needs. Bernard Shaw somewhere says that to a man in the agonies of toothache happiness is the possession of sound teeth. So those who lack adequate food, clothing, shelter, and medical care are apt to define security in terms of the measures required to relieve distress—that is, in terms of a specific program of social security. The prediction that the gratification of need even on this level can never finally be assuaged, that the quest for security renews itself on more complex and higher levels, made all the more poignant by invidious comparisons with the privileges of others, sometimes produces irritation and impatience among those who still suffer from present insecurity. We must never forget that no matter how far we have come from the age of general scarcity, no matter how we measure our affluence, substantial numbers today still live in want below a decent standard of subsistence. To them high discourse about man as a *perennially* needful creature sounds sophistical. It is as if someone were to discount the importance of medical care on the ground that human beings will never be free from some form of ailment, that medical triumphs simply ensure more medical trouble as man's life span is prolonged.

This commonsensical approach, which concerns itself primarily with the degree, scope, and relative intensity of deprivations in physical and social security, in turn provokes the scorn of those who regard the human condition as one of radical insecurity and who interpret the quest for security as an expression of a metaphysical hunger for "cosmic meaning." They are not indifferent to the social insecurities of existence, but they regard them as inconsequential, as distracting chores to be somehow met so that man can confront in stark nakedness the fact of human limitation, and the seal of human finitude, death.

The metaphysical or ontological quest for security is *au fond* a substitute for the loss of religious security which is centered in the belief in God. The existentialists have made it quite apparent that the quest for the *meaning of existence* is a fundamental quest for security. This quest becomes quite acute when the belief is prevalent that, in Nietzsche's words, "God is dead." Whether one accepts or rejects Nietzsche's dictum, it is undeniable that the man who is buoyed up by a belief in a Creator, to Whom he is an everpresent concern, or the man who still retains the attenuated religious belief that the universe or the structure of things is friendly to his hopes and aspirations—has achieved, if not what William James calls "the very sumptuosity of security," at the very least, a security and sense of safety that transcends anything available to those who are not twice-born.

The intimate relationship between religious commitment and the quest for security indicates that we are not dealing with a logical problem alone but with a psychological one. Let us grant that the man who believes he is in the hands of God *feels* a security that cannot be matched by those who regard man as an integral part of Nature and subject to natural laws. Logically this does not speak to man's genuine condition. By definition, God's ways are not human ways. He may destroy man because of his imperfections or humble him as He did Job to test his fidelity. The Author of All Being owes no more to His creatures, perhaps even less, than an ordinary author owes to the characters whom he creates. To suggest anything different is to be guilty of impiety. Even those unconventionally religious men like Emerson and Whitman who accept the world, and believe that man can find security in cheerful affirmation of the natural conditions of his being, must recognize that Nature, with respect to human purposes and human existence, can run amok—that the sufferings produced by the mindless intrusions of fire, ice, flood, and wind in human affairs often dwarf those resulting from human cruelty. Jehovah and Nature are bound by no rules of man.

We must therefore make a distinction between *being* secure and *feeling* secure. The second is not a necessarily reliable index of the first. An entire population can be kept *feeling* secure on serenity pills or other drugs. The fact, however, that such means must be employed is an indication that something is wrong—either objective conditions do not warrant a feeling of security, or if they do, the human psyche is too emotionally disturbed to recognize it. There must be a reasonable relationship between being secure and feeling secure. What that reasonable relation is, is hard to determine without reference to the specification of situations and of personalities caught up in them.

Just as soon, however, as we attempt to discover an *objective* measure of human security we are brought back to the commonsensical, empirical approach which insists that we make a list of human needs in this time and in this place, and ask about the relative progress made in furthering them. When I was very young there were two dread words in common use—"diphtheria," where children were concerned, and "pneumonia" among adults. Security of life to those facing these and kindred threats meant in a very concrete way an increased chance to grow up and survive to a ripe age. No one who is not overly finical can deny that with respect to the generic securities safeguarding men against hunger, disease and death, twentieth-century man has made remarkable strides. One dramatic fact typifies the facts of progress on this plane. Writing just short of a hundred years ago, Karl Marx in *Capital*,[1] to buttress his account of the exploitation of the working class, contrasted the life expectancy of the middle classes and the workers in Manchester and Liverpool. In the first city the average age of death of the middle class was thirty-eight, while that of the workers was seventeen. In Liverpool the comparable figures were

[1] 3 vols.; Chicago: Charles H. Kerr, 1909–1921, Vol. I, p. 704.

thirty-five and fifteen. Today the life expectancy of the entire population in both England and the United States is close to seventy years, with hardly any difference between the middle class and the working class.

Nor is this the whole story. Volumes could be filled with the evidence that with respect to the privations and disasters from which men have suffered in the past, life has become much safer. To be sure, the conquest of new worlds, the opening up of new horizons and dimensions of experience, carries with it risks and dangers previously unknown. In the future, there probably will be multiple hazards in space travel, but the cumulative impact of the scientific skills which make the advances possible will also enable us to reduce these hazards as well as those of present-day automotive travel. Indeed, we already know enough to reduce the latter substantially even now, if we were prepared to pay a sufficient price for it. That human safety and security have a price will always be true in a world of limited resources no matter what economic system prevails.

The cumulative development of the triumph of science, the emergence of what may turn out to be the most far-reaching discovery in the history of man, of what Alfred North Whitehead called "the invention of the method of invention," has given men almost as much power as—but alas!—no greater wisdom than, the gods of Mt. Olympus. The "invention of the method of invention" makes it possible to face the hazards of future discovery with the confidence that they will be met and reduced by greater application and efficiency. The mood of confidence which this generated probably reached flood tide in 1914. What Herbert Butterfield describes in his *Christianity and History* as characterizing the twentieth century as a whole seems to me to be valid only for its early years, and with respect not to the whole of it, to be sure, but to the direction in which things seemed to be moving.

> We of the twentieth century have been particularly spoiled; for the men of the old Testament, the ancient Greeks and all our ancestors down to the seventeenth century betray in their philosophy and their outlook a terrible awareness of the chanciness of

human life, and the precarious nature of man's existence in this risky universe. These things—though they are part of the fundamental experience of mankind—have been greatly concealed from recent generations because modern science and organization enabled us to build up so tremendous a barrier against fire, famine, plague and violence. The modern world created so vast a system of insurance against the contingencies and accidents of time, that we imagined all the risk eliminated—imagined that it was normal to have a smooth going-on, and that the uncertainties of life in the past had been due to mere inefficiency.[2]

Why is it then, despite the increase in the power of man to control his physical environment—shortly before his death von Neumann predicted that man would be able to control certain aspects of the weather!—there is such a widespread feeling of insecurity among human beings *today*? The mood of our culture at home and abroad is one of crisis, uneasiness, uncertainty, and insecurity. The sense of alienation and anxiety seems to be developing almost *pari passu* with the growth of human power. To be sure one might question whether such a judgment could be substantiated, since we do not have anything comparable in the way of firm documentary evidence concerning popular consciousness of past ages. But if what we have said of the psychological role of religion is sound, then the ages of religious faith, which extend to the threshold of our century, must be regarded as ages of greater *psychological* or *emotional* security than our own, despite the physical chanciness of life in those days and despite the lack of an objective warrant for confidence in the great cosmic design.

To what, then, can we attribute our sense of insecurity today? On the whole, I believe we can trace it to the fact that so far we have been unable to extend our power of scientific control to one of the basic social institutions of human culture—war—and to our failure to find moral equivalents therefor. War is not a physical but a social and political phenomenon, and those who have denounced the growth of science and scientific knowledge

---

[2] Herbert Butterfield, *Christianity and History* (New York: Scribner's, 1950), pp. 69–70.

because of its applications to war have no adequate conception of either social causality or human responsibility. Nonetheless, it is true that the very growth in scientific knowledge which has enabled us to limit the devastations of natural catastrophes, like flood and storm, has resulted in *expanding* the scope and intensity of devastation of the social catastrophe of war. The most frightening feature of the arsenal of modern scientific ABC weapons (atomic, bacteriological, and chemical) is that they have wiped out the distinction between combatant and noncombatant. There has been a great deal of hysterical exaggeration about the consequences of war between nations possessing nuclear weapons. We do not know how deadly the effect of such weapons would be if reasonable efforts to safeguard ourselves against them were made or even whether such weapons would be used, and if used, the degrees of their escalation. The statement made by Sir Charles Snow some five years ago that unless there was nuclear disarmament it was mathematically certain the world would be destroyed within the decade, which leaves only five more years to the thermonuclear holocaust, shows that exposure to two cultures does not immunize one from broadcasting alarmist nonsense, and points up the strategic importance for our time of education in the "third culture" of history, politics, and other social studies.

Nonetheless, the very uncertainty and ignorance about these dread things and events lies at the heart of our insecurity. It is sufficient to realize that we live at a time when sudden death is possible, not only for the combatant, but for entire populations. It is true that peace has been guaranteed so far by the balance of terror, and that it *may* be indefinitely preserved, thus enabling most human beings to find surcease from paralyzing fear. After all, people plant crops in the shadow of live volcanoes. But the nagging consciousness of the grim possibilities of nuclear warfare still remains, especially when brush-fire wars are raging. We are justified therefore in concluding that until the ABC weapons are brought under ironclad control by an international authority, our technological age will continue to be marked by a sense of profound insecurity. For in such an age no people can be secure until every people is secure, since even poor nations can acquire lethal weapons, or the wherewithal to make them, on political if not financial credit—and sometimes from the very nations they wish to destroy.

We must have the courage to live with this insecurity as we press for the measures of *multilateral* disarmament necessary to delimit the danger. For whoever wishes to escape the burden of this insecurity is tempted to sacrifice human freedom for the promise of a peace that may be just as deceptive as the peace promised by earlier forms of totalitarianism. Those who are prepared to sacrifice human freedom for security disregard the lessons of history which show that those who surrender their freedom to save their property or their life more often than not end up by losing not only their freedom but their property and life as well. Those who fear the burden of the insecurity required for the defense of freedom owe an accounting to themselves of their debt to those who died defending our present heritage of freedom against previous assaults.

Despite all this I cannot bring myself to believe that the insecurity attributable to the nuclear age is the whole story or even the most important psychological aspect of the problem, granted its primacy in the order of practical priorities. Let us assume that the threats of war, and of civil war, have been allayed. Let us assume further that the computer revolution, the growth of automation, the liberation of nuclear energy on a vast scale for peaceful purposes, and the development of medicine have enabled us to bring the population explosion under control, and ensure, if not a vocation for all who are willing and able to work, a sufficient competence comfortably above the line of poverty. Would this bring the quest for security to a halt? Would man take his ease in a Zion in which machines, instead of slaves, bestow the gift of compulsory leisure on all except irrepressively creative spirits?

This seems to me to be extremely doubtful. It is not necessary to believe that there is something irreducibly metaphysical or transcendent in the constitutions of men which yearns for reunion with the One after a lonely pilgrimage in exile. We can find grounds for this doubt in the restless behavior patterns of contemporary man. No matter how far man's scientific reach will extend, it will always be surpassed by his vision. Patterns of excellence and achievement beyond one's own powers will always beckon, at times even torment, except to those rare individuals who have learned to find contentment, if not happiness, within the confines of their limitations. And who among us can be sure of his limitations until he has made prolonged efforts to overcome them?

Will those to whom life itself is an absolute value be more inclined to surrender it if its span is prolonged? Actually I am not convinced that mere life in its quantitative dimension is itself of value to any reflective person rather than the qualities of experience, the significances and delights of living, which existence makes possible. As I have argued elsewhere, death has its uses, too—often forgotten when prolonged premortal therapy is practiced on those lying helpless on mattress graves. Nor am I prepared to grant that fear of death is biologically innate in man. Men have died willingly for too many causes to make this notion plausible. Fear of death is usually fear of its accompaniments and is bred into man, sometimes so deeply that it becomes the great ally of existing tyrannies. Nonetheless, even if allowance is made for all of the cultural conditioning factors, we cannot discount the tenacity with which men may wish to cling to life when its harshest insecurities have been lightened. It may be more difficult to face death with composure when the world smiles with promise than when it confronts man as a grim and bleak scene inviting hopes of otherworldly compensation.

There are other reasons why the quest for security is likely to be perennial even in our technological utopia. If we define security as escape from risk, we can always reduce risk by reducing the occasions for living. But man is complex and especially so when he seems to be making simple demands. He is a risk-seeking and risk-enjoying creature who at the same time wants to be safe and secure in his adventure. He craves for the excitement of danger even as he seeks the assurance of a happy ending. Give him a world in which there are no risks and it will seem stale and unprofitable to him. He will find occasion to create risks in irrational ways beyond fathoming. One can only make a surmise about its causes, but the facts seem indisputable that for many persons an element of gratuitous risk-taking seems necessary, to give spice and savor to their life. Even children when unobserved sometimes will take breathtaking risks walking the glazed ridges of tenement roofs—not altogether explainable by their childishness—and I daresay it would be difficult to find an adult, no matter how carefully buttoned up he now is, who has not taken some utterly foolish and dangerous risk in the course of his life.

Psychologically we can carry the quest for security too far. Everything in the world may be causally determined, but there are so many independent and plural chains of events intersecting each other that the mind reels at the prospect of the many different ways in which things can go wrong for us even in a well-ordered world. For the number of ways in which things can go wrong is indefinitely larger than the ways they can go right. This is the basis for the promulgation of "Murphy's Law": "If anything can go wrong, it will." One of the disadvantages of a lively imagination is its capacity of envisaging the possibilities of disaster where probabilities cannot be easily determined. Chance plays a much more important role in the biography of men than is commonly realized even when achievement and recognition seem to be the reward of merit alone.

Many of the heroes of this world are heroes of the type of the fabled little Dutch boy whose little finger, stuffed in the hole of the dike, saved the town. Any little boy would have served as well! The conjunction of need and happenstance position defined the situation. And what is true for this kind of fame is also true for some kinds of obloquy. For a naturalistic Pelagian, luck takes the place of divine grace. We fear risks but must take them in order to find our experience satisfying. Perhaps there is a counterpart to the paradox of hedonism in the pursuit of security. Just as the pursuit of happiness is self-defeating so long as we are conscious of striving for it, so the quest for security is self-defeating if we are always impatiently measuring the distance from the object of our quest and appraising possible dangers to it once it seems secured. And just as we often discover happiness after we have immersed ourselves in some work or cause or act of devotion without thought of happiness, so we often find security in running risks and dangers in behalf of projects and goals not immediately relevant to the achievement of personal security. None but a deeply religious man can literally believe that he will find his life by losing it or by throwing it away. But all men know or should know that in the great junctures of life sometimes the *willingness* to lose one's life is our best hope of preserving it, and failing that, of dying with dignity.

There is even a more obvious aspect of security which seems independent at first glance of achievement or triumph over risk. The secure individual is one who enjoys a certain status dependent upon the respect and esteem of the community. He is a person who counts for something and is counted upon by others. There are some strong souls who feel so secure in themselves that they can live without discomfort or anxiety in open and contemptuous defiance of, or indifference to, their fellow men. But most of us are not so sternly self-sufficient. The rebel, the hermit, the recluse, and all others who have gone into internal emigration pay a price for their isolation. It is significant that even they, like so many mindless dissenters and nonconformists today, tend to huddle together in groups in order to reinforce their sense of conformity in dissent. There is no way that I can see of intelligently predicting for the society of the future whether, and how, human beings will become persons of greater concern to each other than they are now. It is not a question merely of receiving justice. Institutional changes can reduce and hopefully abolish injustices. But even if we receive justice, even if men are rewarded according to their merit, they may not feel secure about the outcome. If the affection, esteem, and regard we receive from others depended only upon our intellectual achievements, on our wit or beauty, how many of us would earn it on the basis of pure merit? The profoundest justification of the institution of the family, despite its indictment by thinkers from Plato to Freud, is that it is the best guarantee that human beings will be loved for themselves alone, independently of their talents or merits. There are some simplistic conceptions of human nature according to which the institution of comprehensive social security will resolve all the individual problems at the basis of personal insecurity. But the superficiality of this view is apparent, among other things, from the facts of juvenile delinquency among middle-class groups, and the exaggerated laments about loneliness and alienation among the intellectuals of the affluent societies of the West.

In discussing the quest for security we must always specify the context within which it is sought. We must not speak of security as if "total security" were possible or desirable. A considerable degree of insecurity, in some respects, is tolerable, if some security in *other* respects is assured. In the hierarchy of values each individual must make his own choice. A man who is secure in his love and friendship may even enjoy the insecurities of battle because he knows that defeat does not mean the black despair of the spirit which follows annihilating failure. On the other hand, a man secure in his sense of achievement or power, or in his sense of mission, may be able to live with the uncertainties of the esteem and regard and even affection of his fellows, without troubled concern.

Wisdom and perspective on the human scene suggest an important truth about the economy of human value. This is the inescapable evanescence of value, of any value, either because the capacity for experiencing it withers in time or because one value is limited by other values, and in situations of tragic conflict, must be denied or sacrificed. Charles Peirce, in developing his tychistic philosophy, calls attention to the fact that all things in the world, all values and ideals embodied in human institutions, sooner or later break down. Time and chance take their toll of all our efforts to arrest the flux of things or to escape from it.

There is a point at which every system will fail us. There is a moment when friendship falters, when neither loyalty, love, or faith is strong enough to carry the weight of our expectations. It matters little whether the change is in us or in others. Whatever our virtue, it will some day be found wanting. Whatever our strength, it will some day be surpassed. Nor need this be reason for repining. For it is an integral aspect of the condition of things on which the condition of man depends. To the extent that wisdom depends upon habits of reasonable expectation, we must eschew the unlimited demands we make upon the world, and ourselves, which presupposes that time can stand still or be reversed, that love is eternal, that there are no losers in conflict, or that all problems are necessarily soluble. There is a profound insight in the religious psalms which remind man that there is a season for all things which, even when it is acknowledged, often comes home to man in the actual event with a realizing sense of shock.

From a purely objective point of view no creature who is not self-sufficient or self-caused can ever achieve complete security, for no one can win independence of the conditions of his own existence. The material conditions of determination may be selectively controlled but not suspended. Spinoza's observation that nature may be changed, but only by natural means, reinforces our awareness that we are not omnipotent, that we are inescapably dependent upon natural forces that reck not of human weal or woe and which, for all our scientific triumphs, may overwhelm us. Fear of the unimaginable is irrational but the existence of the unimaginable need not be denied. Psychologically it is absurd *to live* as if the next moment may be our last one, even though it is true that the next moment actually may be our last one. It would be absurd for me to refuse to speak for fear that the next sentence I utter will be my last one. But despite the absurdity of such fear, in fact the next sentence I utter may be my last. This suggests that the facts of insecurity and uncertainty are not themselves the source of dread, but the fears that normally attend our awareness of them.

There is intelligent fear and unintelligent fear. Those who are completely fearless will not live long. Intelligent fear arms us against real dangers and enables us, by modifying the environment or altering our behavior, to reduce the incidence of terror and pain. Intelligent fear must be proportionate to the dangers. It is the absence of any proportion between the danger and the fear which marks the panicky and hysterical response. Political thinking is often distorted by a failure to distinguish between fears that are ill-grounded and those that are well-grounded. This is particularly true about responses to Communism. Those who fear that Communism is a domestic danger and that the republic is about to be subverted by Communist infiltration in high places illustrate unintelligent fear. They bolster these fears with multiple fantasies. But because it is silly to fear Communism as a national danger *in* America, it by no means follows that it is silly to fear it as an international danger *to* America. To see the Supreme Court—and I speak as one guilty of logical contempt of court—as a part of the Communist conspiracy is to be guilty of political psychopathology. On the other hand, to welcome, or even interpret the activities of the Communist Viet Cong and its similars in other countries as a movement of democratic, freedom-loving agrarian reformers is just as much an expression of political psychopathology, and much more dangerous to the survival of free institutions.

Politics aside, my primary point here is that in the general run of our lives, the lives of those who do not make a cult of irresponsibility, we fear too much, too soon, and with insufficient discrimination of the reality, proximity, and magnitude of the dangers that beset the adventure of living. When we learn to be unafraid, the insecure and uncertain loses its terrors for us. And we can learn to be unafraid through habit and reflection. It is a commonplace of human experience that most of the evils human beings fearfully await either never occur—there is a vestigial superstition in people which induces an exaggerated fear of untoward events in order to forestall their occurrence!—or when they do, turn out to be easier to bear than had been anticipated. The greatest evils in experience are the unexpected events which had previously not been feared, and sometimes in the nature of the case, could not have been feared because their nature was not known.

It would be interesting to conduct a survey among those who look back reflectively upon their lives to determine what they regretted most—the things done or the things left undone, the alternatives taken or the chances missed, the habits and routines followed or the ventures and adventures rejected out of fear of the outcome. Although there is an irreducible element of temperamental bias which enters in all such assessments, my observations lead me to the conclusion that human beings have suffered greater deprivations from their fear of life than from its abundance. The most deplorable insecurities are those which prevent human beings from deviating from traditional routines, which prevent them from living their own lives in their own reflective styles. What is required is not Tillich's courage to be, but rather the courage to become, the courage to live in independence of fashion or mere tradition or the judgment of the mobs whose vagaries constitute so much of public opinion.

We must recognize a social responsibility to instate the conditions which make the consequences of desirable risk-taking in human experience less onerous. The principle of insurance has already familiarized us with the conception of shared risk at a fixed but greatly diminished cost to the individual insured. With respect to the untoward events that may strike down an individual through no fault of his own and have a crippling effect on the possibility of recovery, it seems fair to introduce the "socialization of risk." This is the assumption behind the welfare state, which, thankful as we may be for past progress, has still a long way to go to reach a state of genuine welfare. "There but for the grace of God or nature or Lady Luck go I" is a sobering and salutary reflection in a world of contingency and mishap. The multiple revolutions of our time make it technologically and politically feasible, at first in the areas of greatest productivity, to establish a guaranteed floor or level of life below which we should regard it as incompatible with human dignity for a person to sink. The actual level must be a function of social productivity, but once population is stabilized there is no reason to doubt that human ingenuity and effort, especially if enkindled by imaginative identification with others, will be able to wipe out the most crushing forms of poverty and cultural deprivation.

The world will never be completely safe for man, because so long as he has the power of thought and choice, he may choose not wisely but disastrously. There is no substitute for intelligence, but it may not be sufficient. We cannot escape risk, because even an informed choice may be an unlucky one. What responsible person would want it otherwise, would want a world where he was deprived of the power of choice? Even if we could be assured that a lobotomy performed upon us would turn us into angelic zombies with an unmatched feeling of total security, who among us would subject himself to the operation? The grandeur of man consists in this sense of *self*-determination which cannot be dissociated from living with the risks of a world that will always in some respects remain insecure. Men can reduce their insecurities in this world—but life would lose its zest for them if *all* insecurities were to vanish. To be sure, human beings dream of omnipotence when they are frustrated, or when suffering dire need or want. But how dull the world would be if our wishes were not merely father to our thoughts, but the sufficient condition of their realization, if the act followed hard on our very words. If all our wishes came true, then like the child in the fable we would end up by wishing we no longer had the power to wish. For to be without some of the things we want seems necessary to escape *taedium vitae*, that sickness of life which, when it runs deep, has no remedy. There is no need then to lament our human estate of insecurities. Intelligence can help us to reduce some of them, and courage can help us bear the rest with serenity.

Comment by CHARLES H. PATTERSON

Professor Hook has brought to our attention a number of interesting points in connection with man's quest for security. With most of these I am in complete agreement, and hence what I have to say at this time may be regarded as no more than an attempt to supplement what he has presented. Life is indeed a risky affair, and I doubt very much that we would want it to be any other way. While it is true that we are continually striving for security, the fact of the matter is that only a very limited amount of it is either possible or desirable. I suspect that in our present society the ones who have the greatest degree of security are the inmates of our penal institutions. They do not have to worry about food, shelter, clothing, education, war, depressions, or anything else. The government looks after their needs. The only ones who have complete or total security are the people who are dead. But for those who are alive and free to pursue the activities of their own choosing, risk and adventure are of the very essence of their existence. Nothing that is worth while in human life can be achieved without risking something. What hope would there be for a man in business if he was unwilling to risk his time and his money because of the possibility that he might lose? Or what hope would there be for a scholar if he consistently refused to form an opinion on any subject because of the possibility that he might be wrong? The values of life cannot be acquired apart from some dangers, and these dangers must be met and overcome to the best of one's ability.

These observations are trite, but real problems do arise when we are faced with specific threats to our security and we are at a loss to know how to deal with them in the particular situation in which we find ourselves. How, for example, can one hope to have financial security for his old age when the dollars he has been saving for this purpose are constantly shrinking in value? How can one be secure in a world where the threat of a nuclear war becomes more menacing with the increasing development of new means of destruction? How can we protect ourselves against such disasters as the spread of new and mysterious diseases, being deluded by false doctrines, or the failure to bring our appetites and desires under proper control? There is no specific formula that will take care of all these problems. They must be dealt with individually and there is little if anything to be gained by talking about them in general.

There is, however, another problem in connection with our security, and here I think we can say something that will be helpful. It has to do with the selection of those specific kinds of security in which we attempt to reduce the element of risk that is involved. As Professor Hook has pointed out to us, the needs of man are many, and we cannot supply all of them. Some of them are more important than others, and there are instances where the satisfaction of some needs can be achieved only through the sacrifice or giving up of other ones. Which ones should come first? If I can't have security or even a modest amount of it in all areas of life, to which ones should I give the preference? Here it seems to me that what is needed most of all is a method for determining an appropriate scale of values. Obviously, we cannot have everything that is desirable. We are forced to choose between values. It is true that the satisfaction of some needs is a prerequisite for the achievement of others, and it would seem that these should come first. Physical health, financial security, and many other things are means for the achievement of what are usually designated as spiritual values. Freedom from external control by military or governmental coercion is another necessary means for moral and spiritual ends. But of these various means we cannot say that they are of equal importance. I think it will generally be agreed that it is a mistake to sacrifice one's freedom in order to secure economic advantages. And it is also a mistake to regard even life itself as having sufficient worth to be purchased at any price that might be demanded. Means are important, but they are not important enough to warrant the giving up of the ends for which they are the means.

I do not believe that all values are evanescent. Some of them may have a lasting significance that goes far beyond the life span of the individual or even of the race. It is quite possible that they will endure for eternity. These are the ones I would say should not be sacrificed for the sake of values that are merely temporal or of short duration. Intrinsic values are more important than those that are purely instrumental, and those that are in harmony with the welfare of others should always take precedence over the ones that are of advantage to ourselves but can be secured only by the exploitation of other persons. And the acquisition of wealth and power, in spite of their many worth-while advantages, is no adequate substitute for moral integrity. In the competitive society in which we live there is a strong temptation to enjoy the present at the expense of the future and to emphasize material gain over more lasting values. This should be resisted, for a man's life consisteth not in the abundance of the things that he possesses. And what shall it profit a man if he gain the whole world but lose his own soul?

Comment by ROBERT H. HURLBUTT III

Professor Hook's writings are always characterized by the ability to relate philosophical techniques to significant issues in practical life, and this paper is no exception. In a precise and lucid manner, he explores the confused notions of security and their interrelationships. An analysis of this exploration brings to light a series of seemingly incompatible paradoxes wherein security is asserted and denied of the same situations. Modern Western man, for instance, is more secure than his forebears in that his children are less likely to face the disease diphtheria, and yet he is not secure in that he is more likely to face mental disease. Modern man is more secure, in certain countries at least, in that there is less hunger; but, in counter argument, it is claimed that he is insecure in that he has not got rid of war. He is socially secure in the objective senses of less hunger, better medical care, safer shelter, but he nevertheless has to die, or possibly go to hell, or find himself drowning in some other shoreless lake of cosmic insecurity.

Now this sort of dialogue is always confusing; it makes it appear that security is impossible—that for every case of security one can cite a case of insecurity, often produced by the first, as, for example, new scientific discoveries produce increased horrors in war. Thus the counter claims concerning security appear to logically cancel each other out, with the result that it is often asserted that a particular kind of security, say economic security, is unimportant since it will not serve to cure cosmic insecurity. The implication seems to be that there is no circumstance in which a person or a group could be asserted to be unequivocally secure. The term "insecurity" appears to have no contrasting term "security." As the old Kansas City blues song says, "You is so beautiful, but you gotta die someday." Now in response to such gloomy dialectics Professor Hook points out that talk about some cosmic insecurity may blind us to particular sufferings in the form of hunger and disease; he notes that it would be incredibly stupid to stop preventing disease in children because some of those cured later get mental disease; he points out that preoccupation with war as a problem may blind us to the fact that the alternatives to the insecurities of war may be the insecurities of regimented peace, and perhaps even worse. And he quite rightly claims that "total security," if it is possible to give this concept meaning, would produce a tedious, boring, and basically nonhuman state of existence.

It seems to me that a more general difficulty, however, underlies these dilemmas, and I have time only to block it in briefly. I suggest that all or most of such paradoxes are the product of a logical confusion, and that this logical confusion is rooted in an ambivalent way of looking at things which is characteristic of Western man. This ambivalence derives from the attempt to transfer the Christian notion of heaven, a kind of human existence in which there are no problems, to the everyday life span of human beings and to human societies. The mistake might be characterized in the following way—it involves thinking of security as an empty problem-box. Given this sense of "security," man can become secure only by removing all the problems, one by one or in groups, from the box.

Integral to these paradoxes is a vacillation between the notion, on the one hand, of "security" as the predicate of the ability to solve particular problems of a financial, medical, ethical, social, esthetic nature; and, on the other hand, of "security" as the predicate of a situation wherein all problems, actual and possible, are in fact solved. In the latter sense, security is properly asserted, therefore, only when there are no more problems, i.e., when there remains no hunger, pain, disease, anxiety, war, death—no more evils or unpredictables.

That is, security comes when we have removed the last problem from the box, and it is empty.

Now it takes very little thought to see that this is not a viable analogy to life as we all know it to be. As Professor Hook says, there will never be a situation, for either an individual or a culture, when his or its problems, each and every one, are all resolved. To put it another way, if we assume that security comes only when the problem-box is empty, then security becomes impossible, i.e., there will be no actual case in which we could truly assert that a person or a culture is secure. Security, then, in this sense has no practical or empirical meaning.

Once this is recognized, most of the paradoxes Professor Hook investigates tend to disappear. Thus it is simply a logical confusion to argue that although John Jones has economic security in the form of insurance, this security is in some sense negated because he still does not have cosmic security, that is, that he will die someday. He may not be beautiful, either. The fact that he will die does not contradict the assertion that he is economically secure, or that he and others should be. To think that it does is to build anxiety into our lives simply by our way of looking at things.

But there is another sort of confusion generated by the "empty-box" way of conceiving security. It tends to make its holders view all of the problems in the box as of the same kind. Death, for instance, is put on the same logical level as the cure of a specific disease, say infantile paralysis. But death is quite different, in particular in that it cannot be overcome—we may control or vary to some extent the time of its occurrence, or some of its conditions, and these are viable problems; but that it will come we cannot control. And when abstract problems such as the unpredictability of the precise nature of all future events are also included in the box, we have the final impossibility. We cannot put insoluble problems in the box. War is another example of this kind of difficulty—people seem to believe that we can prevent it by finding some simple cause, like a virus in poliomyelitis. Now war is not like a disease in this respect, and in others, and we are not likely to understand its nature, or control its occurrence, so long as we think of it in biological and medical terms. To put it in the problem-box along with things such as particular diseases, however, tends to make us consider it in terms of the same logical categories. Now, if we construe problems in the ways just mentioned, then again we have, so to speak, "built in" the insecurity by our way of looking at life. We have put items in the box that we cannot get out, or we have falsely assumed that all the items in the box are got out in the same manner, and then bemoaned the fact that we have no security unless we get them out.

And, finally, note that even if we were able to get all the problems out of our problem-box, that is, even if we could solve all our problems, and be certain that no more were forthcoming, sneaked in by some dastardly fate, we would still not be rid of one paradox—that security in the form of an empty problem-box is logically equivalent to an empty, boring life. The "security" of a life with no problems would produce the "insecurity" of tedium. Again, however, it is the analogy of security as an empty problem-box that produces the paradox.

Now, what to do. The best suggestion is to get rid of the problem-box analogy; and if this cannot be done, at least the different senses of "security" should be kept separate, and should not be opposed to one another as contradictories. The words "security" and "insecurity" make logical sense only when applied to objects of the same kind, and to the ability to overcome some of the difficulties that plague men. In fact, it appears to me that the word "security" meaningfully relates to particular problems, or kinds or classes of problems, and not to the totality of actual and possible problems. We cannot secularize heaven.

A Sociologist's View

KINGSLEY DAVIS

KINGSLEY DAVIS, professor of sociology and chairman of International Population and Urban Research, University of California at Berkeley, is a specialist in the field of population studies. He was formerly the United States representative on the United Nations Population Commission and is currently the chairman of the Behavioral Sciences Division of the National Research Council. In addition to numerous articles in magazines and professional journals, his works include *Human Society* (1949) and *The Population of India and Pakistan* (1951). He is a former president of both the American Sociological Association and the Population Association of America.

ALAN P. BATES is a professor of sociology and chairman of the department at the University of Nebraska. The Reverend J. FORD FORSYTH, Th.D., is pastor of the First Plymouth Congregational Church in Lincoln, Nebraska.

The word "security," when used by itself, is highly abstract. It means simply that there is some sort of partial protection against some kind of danger for a person or a group. It plainly has a future reference, for the danger is something that *may* happen; and it necessarily involves planning in order to avoid the danger or to compensate for it if it does occur. The degree of protection cannot be absolute, because if there is a full guarantee against a future danger, there is no danger. Complete security exists only in the sense of protection against *certain* consequences of a possible calamity. If *all* undesired consequences are protected against, the calamity will not be a calamity; and if the protection involves overcompensation for the undesirable consequences, the "calamity" will be a benefit. In short, security refers to the degree (short of 100 per cent) to which present planning is able to reduce the probability or lessen the evil consequences of a possible future calamity.

To push the discussion beyond this general level, one has to fill in the specifications. One has to say *whose* security is being maximized, *what* calamity is being anticipated, *which* consequences are being forestalled, *how long* the protection will extend, and by *what means* it will be accomplished. Since each of the specifications can vary over a wide range, the subject is necessarily complicated. In the present paper I intend to look at these questions only in so far as they involve broad sociological or demographic considerations.

Security for What?

Insecurity arises out of life itself, for there is no certainty that the organism's requirements will be met. On top of such biological insecurity, however, human beings have added a multitude of social insecurities. Ironic as this fact may be—because men are the only animals capable of visualizing and planning for the future and because their societies presumably provide more security than solitary existence could provide—the truth is that insecurity is as inherent in the nature of society as it is in the nature of organic life. The reason lies in the peculiar socio-cultural character of human society. For instance, the fact that each society is regulated by communicated patterns rather than by instincts means that the various human societies become mutually unintelligible and hence latently hostile, thus generating external insecurity. Also, by inculcating numerous secondary goals that are competitive and basically insatiable in character—such as prestige, power, wealth—human societies build insecurity into the internal system. This is further developed by the fact that access to the means to all goals is controlled by communicated rules and roles. Although conformity is rewarded and violation punished, the individual's advantage, apart from the sanctions, usually lies in nonconformity, because the rules constrict his means. Since penalties are not certain, the individual constantly balances the gains against the risks of violation. He tends to associate risk with fun, profit, or freedom, and security with caution and boredom. Even when he conforms, however, he may still fear that someone else will eclipse him, by fair means or foul. In such ways human societies generate insecurity.

Strictly speaking, there are only two insecurities concerning goals. One is an individual's ambivalence as to which goals he wants; the other is anxiety over possible failure to attain a goal. The latter is not a question about the goal itself but about the means for attaining it. It is therefore capable of remedy by the application of knowledge and effort, whereas insecurity due to goal-ambivalence tends to paralyze action and is beyond remedy except possibly by inspirational or emotional redefinition. A young man who cannot decide what occupation he wants to pursue is in danger of pursuing none at all that is worth while.

Since human goals and means exist in great variety, so do security and insecurity. In fact, these terms are defined differently according to who is using them. The psychiatrist tends to view insecurity as emotional, irrational, often involving goal-confusion. The theologian looks at it with reference to religious conscience and the next life. The economist looks at it as a financial matter; so important is the financial aspect that a synonym for stocks and bonds is "securities." Also, public policy is concerned mainly with economic rather than other forms of security. The reason that economic security looms so large is not that economic goals are more important than others; it is doubtful that such goals exist except as way stations to noneconomic goals. The real reason is that economics is par excellence concerned with means and especially with means that are scarce and therefore competitive. The distribution of goods and services through an exchange system mediated by money is the master-means of satisfying desires, and of satisfying some people's desires more than others. These are means, furthermore, that are tangible and measurable, hence subject to objective direction and control by public policy. There are, of course, many forms of insecurity which cannot be avoided by economic means—loss of another person's affection, deterioration of mental faculties with age, death, and illness—but in most of these cases some of the unfortunate consequences can be avoided or minimized by economic measures. In sum, the goals themselves are not economic, but the means often are. There is nothing economic about medical care per se—it depends on the physical and biological sciences; but the means of getting medical care are eminently economic. Precisely because it is such a universal means, "economic security" is not really conclusive as to the type of security that is meant. It may mean political security for the nation; it may mean emotional, recreational, medical, or any of a hundred securities for the individual.

Whose Security?

The question "security for whom?" suggests a differentiation between individual security on the one hand and group and societal security on the other. Inevitably, too, it suggests the question of the distribution of security among the individuals and groups within a society. What is called "social security" is for the most part individual security carried out under governmental auspices. By societal and group security, on the other hand, I have in mind the security of organized entities independently of their constituent members. Today we generally think of this in terms of "national security," and when we use the phrase "international security" we mean safety from the danger of war for the various nations composing the international community. The fact that individual and societal security are two different things can be seen immediately when we realize that the one is often sacrificed for the other. A soldier in war is giving up individual security in the interest of national security; a tithing communicant is lessening his own financial security for the benefit of his church. On the other hand, a corrupt official is aiding his individual security at the expense of the collectivity. One of the great human problems is the complex adjustment between social and individual security.

The distributive problem within a society arises from the simple fact that the means to security are scarce. This scarcity is not due to the niggardliness of nature; if anything, nature, especially human social nature, is too profligate. It is due to the propensity of human society to multiply secondary goals of a limitless character. An "abundant society" is merely one that has different scarcities from an impoverished society. In other words, insecurity refers to goals not reached, not to those attained. Security breeds insecurity. At any one time, therefore, a society exhibits a system of striving for goals with scarce means and is faced with the problem of distributing those means.

The distributive problem is separate from but nevertheless related to the question of how much there is to distribute. If an insecure society is one that has very few resources for its members, no system of distribution can itself compensate for this fact. The only way in which the distributive system can affect societal security is by its effect on social efficiency—

mainly economic production and political and military mobilization. It follows that a policy of individual security pursued without reference to the maximization of societal means is a shortsighted policy, with respect both to the majority of individuals and to the collectivity as an entity.

These general observations can be given more concreteness if we turn to particular programs for increasing security in the world today. Let us start by considering the question of development in underdeveloped countries, then go to the campaign to abolish poverty in the United States.

"Freedom from Want" in the Backward Continents

If we accept as a policy the aim of providing greater security for the three-fourths of the world's people (about two and one-half billion) who live in underdeveloped countries, we have to agree that for the moment this policy is succeeding to a remarkable degree. However, its very success is sowing the seeds for its own failure. The paradox is typical: the solution of one problem gives rise to new ones.

Few of us think clearly about policies for underdeveloped countries because of confusion over goals and words. We accept short-range aims that tend to defeat long-range ones. We favor change in one aspect of society but reject it in another, related aspect. We get tangled in semantic obfuscation. For instance, a very old dichotomy between the necessities for human existence on the one hand, and the adornments, luxuries, and miscellaneous dispensables on the other, clouds our vision. The ambiguity between objective and subjective "necessity" allows the basis of the distinction to shift with unnoticed illogicality; and the reality is too complex for a simple dichotomy to be useful (we are actually dealing with a continuum extending from things absolutely required to sustain life to things which, like tobacco and sports cars, are not only unnecessary but harmful).

By way of illustration, one can take the frequent assumption that the impoverished multitudes in the underdeveloped countries "lack even the necessities of life." The implication of the assumption, and perhaps the reason for making it, is that the advanced countries should bend every effort to provide these necessities. The truth is, however, that the backward continents have the essentials of life in greater abundance than ever before. It is precisely for this reason that their populations are growing at an unprecedented rate. Between 1960 and 1965 their population grew at a rate of 2.5 per cent per year[1] which, if continued, would double the number of people every twenty-eight years and increase it tenfold (that is, up to about 25 billion) within ninety-two years. Virtually all of this population growth—never before even approached by any major portion of mankind—has been brought by a decline of mortality. In other words, the essentials of life—freedom from predators, protection from disease, provision of food, clothing, and shelter—have been so abundant that an amazingly low death rate has quickly been achieved, with a resulting unprecedented population growth.

If the underdeveloped areas have the essentials of life, to a degree never approximated before in human history, what is it that they lack? Well, they lack the things that they and others consider desirable for a "decent" level of living. They are things that are subjectively but not actually, or physically, necessary. In other words, the underdeveloped countries are suffering from relative rather than absolute deprivation. Further, they are suffering from insecurity about the future, because it looks as though the present situation—for instance, the extremely low mortality—cannot be indefinitely maintained if other things are not changed. Let us look first at the relative position.

Analysis of national income data for sixty-two countries in 1957 has shown a highly unequal distribution. One-fifth of the total population lives in countries that receive two-thirds of the total income, and 40 per cent live in countries which together

---

[1] Computed by the author from data in United Nations, *Demographic Yearbook*, 1964, pp. 111–112, and *Population and Vital Statistics Report*, October 1, 1965.

receive only 5 per cent of the income. The distribution by quintiles is as follows:[2]

Population	Income (1957)
1st 20%	66.0
2nd ,,	20.5
3rd ,,	8.5
4th ,,	3.0
5th ,,	2.0

Andic and Peacock find that the inequality of the distribution remained about the same between 1949 and 1957, with perhaps a slight tendency to increase. Analyzing subsequent data for both 1958 and 1962, I find that the underdeveloped (i.e., poorer) countries gained in per capita income at only one-fourth the rate shown by the highly developed countries, which suggests that the inequality is widening.

Inequality, however, is only relative. It does not preclude absolute advancement. The truth is that the underdeveloped countries have in general experienced a postwar economic boom since 1945. Andic and Peacock find, among their sixty-two countries, that the three-fifths of the population living in the countries with the lowest income experienced a rise of *aggregate* (*not* per capita) income greater than that of the two-fifths living in the more prosperous countries. The increases were 77 and 34 per cent respectively.[3] Even on a per capita basis, despite their huge growth in population, the less developed countries have improved. I find that in the four years from 1958 to 1962 they gained approximately 5 per cent in per capita income.

Returning to our question of what the underdeveloped countries lack, we see that they lack equality with the developed countries. To what extent the inequality would have to be reduced for them to feel satisfied is impossible to say, but the

[2] Suphan Andic and Alan T. Peacock, "The International Distribution of Income, 1949 and 1957," *Journal of the Royal Statistical Society*, Series A (General), Vol. 124, Pt. 2 (1961), p. 207.
[3] *Ibid.*, p. 209.

very question points to a second source of uneasiness in the underdeveloped countries: The future does not look as though it will bring closer parity. Instead of any progress in the direction of satisfaction, then, one sees only increasing signs of malaise and frustration. The reason for this cannot lie in lack of national gains; we have just seen that the aggregate income gains have been greater in the underdeveloped than in the highly developed countries. The difficulty must lie elsewhere.

To understand what is happening, we need, I think, to avoid lumping all securities into one undifferentiated package, or to treat the "level of living" as if it were a homogeneous category. Coming back to the continuum mentioned above, we can say that the underdeveloped countries have been acquiring the essentials of life to an unprecedented degree but, as a consequence, have been starved of certain other elements in the level of living. Indeed, their progress is grotesquely out of balance. Through a narrow concentration on human beings as sheer animal organisms, the resources of the world have been remarkably successful in meeting the essentials of life in the underdeveloped countries. Death rates have declined in a few years to an extent that took the now developed countries several decades or even centuries to achieve. Mortality has been reduced regardless of whether or not economic development is occurring, and generally with little change in the social structure and hence without institutional changes that would tend to motivate couples to reduce their rate of childbearing. One of the chief experts on world mortality describes the situation as follows:

> Mortality declines which are without precedent in known demographic history have occurred in underdeveloped areas of rapid [economic] growth such as Mexico, moderate [economic] growth such as in Ceylon.... It now seems clear that economic misery as such is no longer an effective barrier to a vast upsurge in survival opportunities in the underdeveloped areas.[4]

[4] Geo. J. Stolnitz, "Recent Mortality Trends in Latin America, Asia and Africa," *Population Studies*, Vol. 19 (November 1965), p. 117. See also *Population Bulletin of the United Nations*, No. 6, 1962 (New York: United Nations, 1963), devoted to "recent trends in mortality in the world."

In many countries the effect of the rapid improvement in mortality and public health has been to increase fertility, because it reduces sterility and spontaneous abortion.[5]

A narrow concentration on the essentials of life (i.e., food, housing, and public health) seems to be self-defeating, a truth seen more clearly by governments in underdeveloped countries than by other nations purporting to help them. Most of the underdeveloped countries still have resources adequate to give greater immediate economic security to all segments of their population, but they do not do so because they wish to use some of their resources for other things. They are not callous; they are simply trying to get economic development, which requires that their citizens be trained, organized, and motivated to work more productively than in the past. These nations must fend off the immediate pressure to consume in order to make long-run capital investments. They must also contend with another problem—high rates of reproduction—which requires drastic means to deal with. The motivation to acquire training, to work, and to keep reproduction within bounds is not automatic. It has to be generated by specific institutional arrangements comprising a system of penalties and rewards. An arrangement whereby the necessities of life are guaranteed regardless of an individual's performance is one that, in a poor society, produces more poverty. It even tends to break down whatever institutions in the old system motivated productive effort. A policy that thinks only in terms of providing basic security to all, with no provision for productive effort and population control, seems likely to fail. Most underdeveloped countries recognize this in practice, but welfare theory often overlooks it.

An exclusive emphasis on physical necessities also overlooks the fact that human beings are not satisfied with such necessities alone. As participators in complex societies organized on the

---

[5] Evidence of a recent substantial rise in age-specific fertility rates in eleven countries of Latin America is given in O. Andrew Collver, *Birth Rates in Latin America: New Estimates of Historical Trends and Fluctuations* (Berkeley: International Population and Urban Research, 1965). Similar evidence has been found for Jamaica, Ceylon, and several other countries.

basis of symbolic communication and elaborate social conditioning, they will invariably sacrifice some of their organic needs and satisfactions in behalf of psychic ones. Given the fact that the social system in turn requires other things than the sheer physical survival of its members, we can see how superficial a policy concerned chiefly with "providing the basic necessities for all" can be.

THE ANTI-POVERTY CAMPAIGN IN THE UNITED STATES

If preoccupation with physical survival is a defect in backward countries, it is worse in highly developed ones. The overwhelming majority of people in the latter countries can provide themselves with both the necessities and some of the adornments of existence. The remaining small minority, helpless or unproductive for some reason, can be provided with the necessities and something beyond through schemes of public aid. Life is so safe in the United States, for example, that under the health conditions of 1963 the average person lives to age seventy, and 89 per cent of those born would reach age fifty.[6] The diseases people die of are mostly those associated with old age, and they are brought on more by the superabundance of the economy than by its poverty. Questions concerning the distribution of the means for security thus hardly concern physical survival, although they are confusingly phrased that way. They concern rather the problem of economic security as a right versus economic security as a reward. This is an old problem made more complex by two features of advanced societies: the limitless quality of "security" when it is divorced from physical necessity, and the thinly disguised use of force by organized groups within these societies to increase their share of security. The anti-poverty movement in the United States illustrates these problems. The propaganda accompanying the movement, for example, exploits the typical ambiguity of the goal. The cover of a 1962 booklet on *Poverty and Deprivation in the United States*[7] proclaims that 77 million

[6] U.S. National Center for Health Statistics, *Vital Statistics*, 1963, Vol. 2, Sec. 5, pp. 5–7.

[7] Washington, D.C., Conference on Economic Progress.

people in this country are *either poverty-stricken or deprived.* Taken in one sense, this estimate is absurdly conservative. There were in 1962 about 187 million Americans, and all of them were "deprived." Taken in another sense, the statement is a misrepresentation, because it implies that the richest nation in the world has 38 million people, a fifth of its entire population, who are "poverty-stricken" and thus lacking the essentials for existence. A glance back at history will show the distortion contained in this "statistic," which unfortunately obscures the real problems.

Between 1870 and 1955, per capita real income in the United States multiplied itself more than six times.[8] Between 1955 and 1963 it continued to climb, gaining by more than 20 per cent in eight years.[9] Also, the distribution of income has shown a tendency to equalize itself. In 1929 the lowest two-fifths of families and unattached individuals received only 12.5 per cent of the total family personal income, whereas in 1963 they received approximately 16 per cent.[10] (This equalization tendency is, of course, greater when after-tax income is taken.)

It follows that most of the people in the lowest fifth of the income scale now are receiving a higher real income than the rich received in the earlier history of the United States. To put it differently, we are now nearly all rich. Utopia is already here. If we continue to wring our hands, surely the problem is not "dire poverty," except in a few cases. It must be something else.

A similar conclusion is reached when we compare the United States with poorer nations. In 1962 our per capita income was forty-three times that of Uganda.[11] It would be hard to find anybody in the United States who has as low an income as the average Ugandan. By Ugandan standards, nearly everybody in the United States is rich. Since most of the world has a very

[8] *Historical Statistics of the United States from Colonial Times to 1957* (Washington: Bureau of the Census, 1960), p. 139.

[9] Census Bureau, *Current Population Reports, Consumer Income,* Series P-60, No. 43 (Sept. 29, 1964), p. 3.

[10] *Ibid.,* p. 9.

[11] *Yearbook of National Accounts Statistics,* 1963, Table 3A.

low per capita income compared to ours, it follows that the great majority of those arbitrarily placed in our so-called "poverty" group would be wealthy by world standards. Surely the three-fourths of the world's people who still live in poor agrarian countries must look on in astonishment while we complain about our impoverished millions. Perhaps they wonder why we ship surplus wheat abroad and charge our "poor" forty cents for a loaf of bread.

My purpose is not to belittle a concern for economic security for those Americans who have less of it than the great majority, but to open our eyes to the exaggerations that damage such a concern. We are implicitly given to understand that a broad segment of our population is suffering from lack of physical necessities when in fact they are overwhelmingly suffering from relative deprivation. Even when this is recognized, the reporting tends to be slanted so as to denigrate our achievements. The United States Department of Commerce states:

> The lowest 20 per cent of the families in the United States today may have higher standards of living than the highest 20 per cent had 50 years ago. They may also have better food, clothing, and shelter and greater life expectancy that the top income groups in many other parts of the world. This fact, however, provides little consolation when they see how little they have in comparison with their neighbors.[12]

The author dismisses the greatest achievement of human history (the industrial revolution) and singles out as more important a universal trait of human nature—envy.

A definition of "poverty" as relative deprivation raises the question of the fairness and efficiency of the income distribution scale. There is nothing wrong with this question, but it is quite different from the problem of absolute deprivation and should not be confused with it. Also, any usable definition of poverty in relative terms must be objective; it must state the degree of inequality that constitutes poverty. As long as this point is left

[12] *Trends in the Income of Families and Persons in the United States* (Washington: Bureau of the Census, 1963), p. 2.

indefinite or left as a matter of subjective feeling, there can be no elimination of poverty. Short of absolute equality of income —which no society has achieved—one can never get rid of a feeling of deprivation on the part of those who get less. One cannot abolish the lowest section of a distribution curve. Eliminate the lowest fifth, the next fifth is then the lowest, and so on. Only when poverty is defined objectively in terms of the degree of inequality—say, as an income less than one-fifth of the average income—can any thought of eliminating it be intelligible. Even then there is no likelihood of getting rid of the psychological dissatisfaction brought on by having less than one's neighbors.

To speak only of poverty in a present sense, even in the most informed way, says little about the question of economic security. Since security refers to the future and to what one can count on, a person who is poor by some definition may nevertheless be secure. He may be able to count on having in the future whatever he has today. Since most people will trade some current returns for surety of future returns, any policy respecting the economic situation of the poorer strata should deal with the question of future security as well as future opportunity. By their very nature, opportunities are greatest where risks are greatest. The task of providing the poor with avenues to better their situation is therefore a different task from that of minimizing their risk.

The security of the relatively poor segments can be increased either by somehow reducing their current poverty and letting them use the gains themselves for the purpose of maximizing their own security, or it can be done by providing them with forms of security which they could not manage either at current or at improved levels of income. Let us consider the first approach. It can be accomplished either by raising the *absolute* level of income of the poor or by improving their *relative* position. To raise their absolute level does not require changing the income-distribution pattern at all; it simply requires raising the income of all classes—that is, the income of the entire society. On the other hand, even if the national income remained constant, the level of the lower strata could be raised by changing the ratio of their income to that of other classes. These are not mutually exclusive alternatives. Historically, in the United States as well as in other advanced industrial countries, both processes have been at work. But the gains for the lower-income groups have been greater through upgrading the entire population than through collapsing the income scale. If, in 1961, the total personal income of the United States had been distributed equally to all families and unattached individuals, the lowest fifth of the income-receivers would have had its income raised four and three-tenths times.[13] This would have been a smaller gain than was actually made historically between 1870 and 1955, when, as noted already, income rose more than six times. Admittedly the historical period taken embraces eighty-five years, but on the other hand the equalization posited—absolute equality—is very drastic. I believe that general economic growth is a more potent means of improving the lower classes than is income redistribution. General growth also has the additional advantage of being able to act continuously, whereas income redistribution, once accomplished, cannot be repeated (except in reverse). It follows that if equalization of income should somehow slow or reverse the rate of economic development, it would in due course constitute a threat rather than a benefit to the poor.

Four classic ways in which income-equalization may theoretically depress the rate of economic growth are as follows: (1) undermining the incentive system for innovation and productive effort; (2) lessening the ability of the social system to select for talent; (3) reducing the power of the economy to generate investment capital; and (4) removing the restraints to population growth. Curiously, however, the same effects have been claimed to flow from a high degree of inequality of income.[14]

[13] Computed from *Statistical Abstract of the United States, 1963*, Table 449, p. 337.

[14] Rigid stratification may lead to a waste of talent, because the elite do not need to exert themselves and the poor have no opportunity to do so; it may also discourage investment, because the elite spends its funds

If both sets of deductions are true (and I think they are), it means that they are arguing the effects of extremes—extreme equality or extreme inequality of income—and the assumption must then be made that there is, for any given stage of technological evolution, an optimum degree of economic inequality that lies somewhere between the extremes—far from zero on the one hand and far from the maximum possible on the other.

The Anti-Poverty Campaign and the Production of Children

The goal of the anti-poverty campaign is not clear. It means different things to different factions and therefore has a wide emotional appeal that would be lost if its purpose were rigorously defined. For the most part, however, the aim of "eliminating poverty" seems to be more of a utopian slogan than an operational policy. The policy seems in fact to be an effort to help certain poor people. Put in this simple way, the campaign must wrestle with an age-old problem: how to deal with persons at the lower rungs of the social ladder in such a way as to avoid making them ever more dependent on such help. The "poor" are not homogeneous. Different kinds of people low in the income scale must be considered separately. To the degree that a society is open, the adult poor have already had a chance to help themselves. If they have not seized the opportunity or if they have fallen from higher rungs in the social scale, the difficulty may lie in their own handicaps. Some of these handicaps may be insuperable; this is true in the case of many impoverished adults. Sizable numbers of them suffer from defects—such as mental retardation, mental disease, old age, chronic alcoholism, drug addiction, poor health, lack of education—which are either impossible to remedy or remediable only at great cost and effort. They require relief administered

---

for luxury and the poor keep their assets completely liquid. See the author's paper, "The Role of Class Mobility in Economic Development," *Population Review*, Vol. 6 (July 1962), pp. 67–70.

in such a way as to take into account their particular problems; they cannot be expected to provide their own economic security, but on the other hand, they in turn cannot be expected to be freed from all relative economic disadvantage. Of course the handicaps of some poor adults are remediable; such individuals can be rendered more competent to provide for their own future security and to participate in collective security arrangements, such as pension plans, that are related to their productive activity. It must be clear, however, that the degree to which there are goods and services to be provided depends on the rate at which they are produced. While an industrial society can certainly take care of its dependents—the old, the young, and the chronically ill—in a decent way, it cannot afford to promise security in abundance independently of the contribution made to the economy by people who are capable of making such a contribution. One of the clearest examples of economic decay from politically rather than economically motivated security was Argentina under the Peron regime. The Soviet Union, in contrast, has long had to cut back its promises and stress rewards for output. It has instituted sharp wage differentials. It has attempted to strengthen the role of factory managers. It has decreased one great class of "dependents"—wives—by insisting that they join "the productive labor force."

In the last analysis the children of the poor are the great hope of the anti-poverty campaign. They are the ones who can most readily profit from the new opportunities presented to them. The one great difficulty is that unless something very powerful intervenes, they will tend to suffer from the crippling circumstances of their parents. There is no way to avoid this tendency as long as the family remains the reproductive and child-rearing institution, as it doubtless will.[15]

---

[15] Obviously, not all of the poor are born into poverty. An open society necessarily has downward as well as upward mobility. Persons near the bottom of the economic scale come in some degree from all classes. In so far as people move downward in the social hierarchy, their problem is not lack of opportunity, for they had this in abundance to start with. The children of the poor, on the other hand, are disadvantaged from the start.

This fact gives us pause. How can family influence in impoverished circles be minimized, at least with respect to the perpetuation of crippling attitudes and characteristics?

One way to view the matter is in regard to the very production of children itself. In giving a reward to people, a viable society expects in return some effort or contribution by the individual at some time in his life, in some way congruent with what he receives. Our implication up to now has been that this is economic—the contribution being production and the reward income. However, the services and disservices that people render, and the rewards they receive, are not all economic. One of the greatest of the noneconomic activities is childbearing and child-rearing, and it is rewarded in noneconomic ways. Interestingly enough, reproduction is not a specialized activity but one engaged in by the great majority of the population. For this reason, the question of oversupply, with the attendant question of overrewarding, is more relevant than it is with respect to purely economic activities. Further, how does reproductive activity relate to the economic system; particularly to income inequality, and poverty? Briefly, my view is that the population as a whole—even in industrial societies—produces an oversupply of offspring and that the poor, to their own disadvantage, do so to a greater degree than other groups (though not by such a margin as once was the case). Furthermore, it is not merely the amount of reproduction among the poor that constitutes a handicap to them but also the circumstances under which it occurs. The difficulty impinges most on the children, youth, and young adults—the ones whose prospects for help are otherwise most hopeful. It is not just a matter of the family's ability to support children, but also a matter of the erosion of ability itself.[16]

There is a common impression that the inverse relation between income and births has disappeared, but in fact it has

[16] See the writer's paper, "Some Demographic Aspects of Poverty in the United States," in Margaret Gordon (ed.), *Poverty in America* (San Francisco: Chandler Publishing Co., 1965), Ch. 21. The facts given in the next few paragraphs are from this chapter.

only lessened. In 1960 the average wife aged thirty-five to thirty-nine had borne the following number of children:

Family Income (1959)	Children Ever Born (by 1960)
Under $2,000	3.7
$2,000–7,000	2.9
$7,000+	2.5

The wives with family incomes of under $2,000 in 1959 had borne a higher number of babies at every age than had the wives of all other income classes combined. At age twenty to twenty-four they had borne 13.3 per cent more; at thirty-five to thirty-nine, they had borne 24.1 per cent more. The excess is greater at older ages, because the wives of the poor less consistently or effectively use birth control. It doubtless works the other way too: some wives are in the low-income group because they have had so many children. In any case, there is no doubt that the above-average reproduction of the poor makes them poorer on a per capita basis and gives their children a poorer start than would otherwise be the case.

For families in which the wife is aged thirty-five to thirty-nine, the "under $2,000" group had approximately $282 per person; the "$10,000–14,999" group, $2,856. The spread in *per capita* income is 10.1 times, whereas in sheer *family* income it is only 8.3 times.

In other words, excess reproduction in the poorest households tends to subject the next generation to poverty conditions in greater degree than is called for by the existing distribution of income. This can be seen in various ways. For instance, a disproportionate share of the next generation is being reared by undereducated women. Among ever married women aged thirty-five to thirty-nine in 1960, those with only an elementary education or less constituted 21.9 per cent of the total group but had 26.4 per cent of the children reported for the group. Among nonwhites in the population, the excess reproduction of the poorest families is particularly noticeable. For wives aged thirty-five to thirty-nine in 1960, the differentials were as follows:

	Children Ever Born		Indices	
	White	Nonwhite	White	Nonwhite
Under $2,000	3.32	4.43	100	100
2,000–7,000	2.81	3.28	85	74
7,000+	2.48	2.47	75	56

It is hard to avoid the conclusion that a factor in the poverty of low-income nonwhite families is their reproduction, and that one way in which upper-class nonwhite families achieve and maintain their status is by a low rate of reproduction.

Now let us recall that poor people in our country tend to penalize themselves and perpetuate their poverty by the circumstances as well as the amount of their reproduction. That illegitimacy is more common among the poor is suggested by the fact that about 35 per cent of all illegitimate children not adopted are receiving public relief funds, whereas only about 3 per cent of legitimate children are doing so. Also, the illegitimacy rate is high for very young mothers. According to 1962 estimates, one out of every five illegitimate births occurs to a mother under eighteen, which means that conception for the most part occurred at sixteen or younger; but only one out of thirty legitimate births occurred to a mother that young. An association of illegitimacy with poverty is further suggested by the fact that the nonwhite illegitimacy ratio is greater than the white. In 1962 nonwhites accounted for 11.6 per cent of the total U.S. population but for 61.2 per cent of the illegitimate births.

Curiously, illegitimacy is increasing. The estimated illegitimate births per 1,000 unmarried women aged fifteen to forty-four has tripled since 1940, from 7.1 in that year to 21.5 in 1962. In the latter year the birth rate among unmarried women was more than one-seventh of what it was among married ones.

Although young girls have more illegitimate births (74 per cent of births to girls under fifteen are illegitimate), the fastest rise in the illegitimacy rate has been among women aged twenty-five to thirty-four. This, plus the fact that the proportion of illegitimate births that are of higher order has been rising, suggests that in some social strata, illegitimacy is becoming chronic.

Illegitimate Births That Are:	Per Cent 1947	1962
First Births		
White	73.7	62.6
Nonwhite	52.0	39.6
5th Births and Above		
White	3.6	8.2
Nonwhite	9.9	21.1

Another circumstance affecting the poor more than others is early marriage—often, like illegitimacy, a product of illicit conception. By taking all first births and assuming a fifth of these to be premaritally conceived (as is found generally in the U.S.) we can add these to the illegitimate births to get what I call the "social tragedy conception rate." This rate in 1962 was more than double the illegitimacy rate, being 47.5 per 1,000 unmarried women.

An early age at marriage is associated with a low educational level but with a high rate of reproduction. Also, early marriages tend to reduce the labor-force participation of women, not only by making them wives but also because the early marriers participate, as wives, less in the labor force during the first years of marriage than do wives who marry later. Also, premature marriage is an important cause of school dropouts for both men and women.

The economic opportunities of the children of the poor are thus jeopardized in several ways—first, by the tendency of their parents to have more children than they can cope with and to have them under adverse circumstances; secondly, by the tendency of the children themselves, in greater degree than more economically advantaged children, to get involved in illegitimate pregnancy, early marriage, and early childbearing, all of which lessen their capacity to take advantage of career opportunities provided by the society. The society is not in need of a high rate of reproduction. It needs skills more than bodies. All economic classes are reproducing at a high rate. The nation may well look to ways to discourage such a high rate of reproduction and such damaging patterns of family formation among the poor. If a policy is pursued which allows these features to continue but merely renders them less hazardous for the poor, the result will be to encourage disadvantageous behavior. It is a dubious policy to reward girls financially for illegitimate pregnancy when legitimate pregnancy is costly; it is reckless to encourage young people to marry when they cannot support a family. It is illogical to pursue a program of avoiding school dropouts at the same time that grade school and high school pupils are allowed to marry and incur the obligations of parenthood.

Conclusion: The Balancing of Goals in the Quest for Security

Reflection on what has been said will make clear, I think, that the quest for security inevitably involves the question of different and competing goals. The failures of the present and the problems of tomorrow tend to arise from the fact that in developing the means of achieving one goal, societies unwittingly damage another. For example, the present concern with underdeveloped areas tends to be phrased too exclusively in terms of physical survival. The very success in giving people in these areas the essentials of existence has led to a self-defeating population increase and a new kind of widespread poverty—the poverty of people who remain alive but do not have much to live for. Similarly, the effort to "abolish poverty" in the United States has been accompanied by propaganda which again paints the problem as a lack of absolute necessities. Even when the problem is stated to be one of deficient opportunity for the disadvantaged strata, there is often a failure to recognize that opportunity cannot be wholly made *for* people. The nearest place it comes to being made for one is in the family, when one is a child. In the larger community opportunity is merely a chance to advance oneself by doing something that contributes to the economic life of the society. To do something, to contribute to productivity, takes more than the opportunity itself; it takes skills and work. If the incentives for these are not acquired at home, it is very hard for them to be instilled anywhere else. Also, the crucial period for getting ahead is in adolescence and early adulthood, when lifelong decisions are made. For these reasons, sizable families in which children can receive little parental attention, and involvement of adolescents in illicit reproduction or premature marriage, are ways in which the poor tend to handicap themselves and perpetuate their poverty, regardless of opportunity in the community at large. A campaign to cut the transmission of poverty from parent to child cannot ignore familial and reproductive patterns if it is to succeed.

There are many other examples of how the quest for security in one sphere is frustrated by competing goals, ignorance, or taboos in another sphere. Anyone who publicizes such cases is courting unpopularity, but it is only by assessing all significant influences that a community can learn what to risk and what to sacrifice in the present for the purpose of survival in the future.

Comment by ALAN P. BATES

The word "security" is not only highly abstract; it is also a word which nearly everyone feels he understands without having taken time for careful reflection on its meaning. Kingsley Davis's analysis of the term is consequently really illuminating and helpful in the context of this symposium. So too is his distinction between individual and societal security, because it aids us to see that under some circumstances to stress security for the one is to forego or reduce it for the other. The distinction forces our attention in a new way on some of the burning public issues of the time. Introduction of the familiar sociological concept "relative deprivation" is a third conceptual clarification useful in thought about the problems of security.

With these and other ideas as tools Professor Davis raises hard and penetrating questions about the usual level at which public discourse concerning security is pitched. The perspective from which he writes, it should be made clear, is that of the trained sociological analyst. It is not a paper in social ethics, although of significant import for ethics. Within the confines of his paper, Davis is neither "for" nor "against" the poor, for example. What he has to say, nevertheless, might well be required reading for persons charged with developing programs for increasing the security of less fortunate people.

For all of its intellectual challenge and potential utility there are, in my view, two misinterpretations of the paper a careless listener or reader might make. The first is the notion that its author is promulgating a conservative social philosophy which derides all humanitarian impulses and programs, that he is a twentieth-century incarnation of the viewpoint that earned nineteenth-century economics the label "gloomy science." Actually, Kingsley Davis's social philosophy is unknown to me, and I do not believe it can be found in his paper. My concern is that his analysis not be labeled a plea for any social philosophy, but rather seen as a conceptual analysis supported by evidence of conditions relevant for all social philosophies. He is discussing facts of life and pointing out some of their implications, but he leaves plenty of room for philosophical differences about policies concerning these facts.

Consider the distinction between individual and societal security. In a democratic society, when the security of the individual is in conflict with collective security we are likely to find heated public controversies. In such debates the positions taken are very often predetermined by strongly held political and social philosophies rather than by a clear grasp of the real issues and the relevant evidence. To all such combatants it seems to me that Professor Davis is saying, "Do not let your philosophical views, your ignorance of the facts, or short-run political considerations blind you to the hard, unyielding realities that lie below the surface of the debate."

This is the only plea he is making, I believe. In making it, he is perfectly well aware as a sociologist that in many concrete circumstances philosophical views, an inadequate supply of facts, and short-run political considerations are also realities, and this leads me to the second possible misinterpretation of his paper. Some may suppose that Professor Davis would hold in contempt all ethical or perhaps religious views which take into account factors not dealt with in his analysis. In this instance one would be assuming not that he has an antihumanitarian bias but that he feels he has set forth *all* the considerations necessary for a wise determination of public policy in matters of personal and societal security. In my opinion he would hold that the points he makes should be considered by anyone realistically thinking or acting about security, but I feel sure that he would recognize that questions of human security can meaningfully be discussed from other perspectives than his.

Perhaps I can make my point about other perspectives clearer by further reference to the notion of relative deprivation. We grasp the idea contained in the words easily because it conforms to the experience of all of us. In the academic world those of us who have to recruit staff know very well when we ask for higher professorial salaries that professors are not starving. But they are comparing their salaries with those in other institutions where they might seek employment, or comparing the financial rewards of professors in general with those of nonacademic professionals. They compare and they feel deprived. Their deprivation, objectively viewed, is only relative, to be sure, but the experience of deprivation is nonetheless real and furthermore, nonetheless economically significant.

Professor Davis points out that the poor in America today are only relatively poor and that some are indeed better off than the rich were yesterday. There are still parts of the world where men might count no price too high which would secure for them and their families the diet which millions of Americans (some "poor" among them) casually give to their animal pets. When all we take into account is this sort of comparison, it would seem that the economically disadvantaged in this country hardly deserve our sympathy. But the accuracy of Professor Davis's analysis need not and should not lead us into oversimplification and easy cynicism about either the motives of men or the goals of a society.

Speaking only in economic terms, we may say that the wheels of the economy continue to turn in part because millions of men and women feel deprived and in fact are deprived relative to others. Relative deprivation is the other side of a coin labeled "achievement motivation." It is in the interest of the economy that our society reduce to the absolute minimum the number of those people who cannot feel and respond with effective effort to this motivational fuel for social stability and growth. That is why an "antipoverty" program, despite an antiquated, misleading rhetoric, may, if otherwise soundly conceived, contribute to both individual security and the security of the society. What is valid in such programs is badly put by its protagonists, it is true. Surely the American people can understand and support a more accurate delineation of the objectives of programs designed to increase security. Outworn shibboleths are sacred to politicians and publicists, but from time to time they must be abandoned for more adequate formulations.

In the ethical sphere the clarifying notion of relative deprivation should not lead to a relaxation of social idealism. It is indeed a great victory that almost no one starves in America today. But we do have millions of citizens living under conditions which really block the development of their full capacities as human beings. From one point of view they are only relatively deprived. Nevertheless, they are a wastage and a loss both to themselves and to society. As long as this is true, a significant moral challenge is presented to each relatively well-off American, to each community, and to society at large. So long as the fundamental institutions of the society are not threatened by the remedial actions we take, we should never cease our efforts to bring greater abundance and security to those who are relatively deprived.

Professor Davis does not explicitly disavow either of the possible misinterpretations I have discussed, nor is he under any obligation to make clear all of the things he is *not* saying. I have tried to do so in these two instances because many people are unacquainted with the intellectual posture of the professional analyst of society. Confronting even a distinguished sample, as in the present instance, there may be a failure to recognize it for what it is, and a desire to determine whose axe (hopefully one's own) the man is grinding. No axe is being ground, but Professor Davis has contributed a clear, dispassionate analysis of a complex social problem.

Comment by the Reverend J. FORD FORSYTH, Th. D.

Ministers may often be accused of stepping in where sociologists fear to tread. The ministry and the church are forced into this position because we rarely deal with people statistically, but in day-to-day arrangements of their lives, and of their relationship to one another in the community. We enter the search for security first of all in a very personal way. Through the ages religion represents one of the ways in which men have searched for security. I would propose that a symposium of this kind could well include a paper of full length dealing with man's quest for security from the theological point of view, from the religious point of view.

In the quest for security through religion, the emphasis has tended to be upon the individual. We have lifted up the individual in his dignity and sought to serve him. We have recognized that it is not always economic security which provides the personal security. Dr. Davis commented, "A person who is poor by some definition may nevertheless be secure." My mind goes back to the first mission field in which I served, where Bertie and his family came each Sunday morning to church in a little schoolhouse. Bertie was a transplant from the cockney district of London. His economic situation was deplorable in terms of much of his environment. Yet Bertie, with real happiness, drove his ox over seven miles, dragging a cart with his family in it, to attend worship on Sunday morning. I knew no one in that whole mission field who had a greater sense of security than did Bertie. Yet I could not, as a minister, say that his security was the ideal of the church. The Protestant ethic has tended toward emphasis upon the individual, but in many ways this individualistic ethic has now been shattered. The church today is faced with the same problems that the sociologist faces in society. We are responding to it in varied ways. One of the ways is to listen to the sociologist and his analysis! The modern church is interested in "the world" to a degree which makes uncomfortable many parishioners in our churches. We have discovered that not only must we produce an individual ethic, which seems now often to be in the discard, but that we must also find some way of contributing to a societal ethic. Only as one can achieve both of these is there the opportunity for something of Dr. Hook's definition of security.

We face in the church the question of population control. Churchmen differ in their approach to family planning but I think not in their concern. I believe as we consider the overpopulation problem, so sharply brought to our attention by Dr. Davis, we may as a religious community define more clearly the meaning of personhood and understand that we have a responsibility for personhood before conception takes place.

As a religious community we are concerned with goals and purposes which cannot be defined in economic or in political terms. We cannot, however, escape the need for economic and political action. We expect persons to have individual convictions and to have the courage to act upon them and therefore often to risk some of their security in order that they may be persons of integrity. We have a concern that there will be for all people the opportunity to reach through to integrity of purpose, to acceptance of goals and commitment. It is easy for us to twist "The Lord is my Shepherd, I shall not want," into "The Lord is *your* Shepherd, *you* shall not want," which is a travesty, of course, of religion. In an open society, Dr. Davis said, the poor have already had a chance to help themselves. He qualifies the statement, but I hold it up because I believe the church moves with a conviction that society has not been sufficiently open. The "poor" have not had the opportunity to help themselves in the measure that may be necessary to bring forth their service and encourage fruitfulness in society.

The church, and I as a minister, believe in the voluntary

principle. We do seek to move into the life of an individual person, and also to help that person to see life together, to see himself in relation to the great institutions of our society—family, church, school, government—and to accept his place responsibly in the midst of them. We seek a life affirmation. We hope to create within the individual the motivation, of which again Dr. Davis spoke, to acquire training, to work, to keep population within bounds, to enjoy creative leisure and to find the moral strength which inevitably must be part of the security which makes a good society.

A Psychiatrist's View

HOWARD P. ROME, M.D.

Dr. Howard P. Rome, president of the American Psychiatric Association, heads the Section of Psychiatry at the Mayo Clinic, Rochester, Minnesota. A consultant to the Surgeon General, he has served as president of the Mental Health Film Board (1959–1961), as chairman of the Special Medical Advisory Group of the Veterans Administration (1960–1961), and on the Council of the National Institution of Mental Health. Dr. Rome was also chairman of the American Medical Association's Section of Nervous and Mental Diseases, as well as editor of the American Lecture Series in Clinical Psychiatry and of the *Journal of Religion and Mental Health*.

Dr. Robert J. Stein is a practicing psychiatrist and clinical associate professor of neurology and psychiatry, College of Medicine, University of Nebraska. Dr. Merrill T. Eaton, who holds a professorship on the same faculty, is Clinical Director of Adult Outpatient Services at the Nebraska Psychiatric Institute.

Man's quest for security is a series of epic dreams that reflect the heroic proportions of his social organization and testify to his personal struggles with anxiety and power—the leitmotifs of death that prompt the quest. The trail of these experiences leads through a labyrinth of psychological development, and its homologues in cultural myth, folklore, political organization, and the shadows they cast on the literature of the times.

The record which is left is an odd assortment. It is a mixed bag of cryptically voiced hopes and aspirations. Often they are expressed in fantasy—that half-cloaked imagery which masks as much as it reveals and thus hidden looks at two worlds: one, a world of reality, the source of its raw perceptual data; the other a world of wishful thinking that uses reality as a springboard with which to leap to the fulfillment of hope unfettered by time, logic, or circumstance.

One must follow several paths to explore the traces of the quest for security in each of these worlds. In the world of fantasy, security aspires to a metaphysical state that surpasseth understanding. The way to it has been called brilliant, illuminated by the dreams of old men and the visions of young men. Fantasy has a luminous history, brightly lit by the radiant prophecies of visionaries. It contrasts sharply with the mundane gropings "through the darkness of mental life," as Freud termed man's struggles in the world of reality.[1]

Only the language of metaphor is sufficiently facile to express the polychromed ideas that color "the tangled bank of life, the

---

[1] Sigmund Freud, "Some Elementary Lessons in Psychoanalysis," *The Standard Edition of the Complete Psychological Works of Sigmund Freud*, trans. James Strachey (London: Hogarth Press, 1953–1964), II, 286.

web of thought," to use Hyman's phrase.[2] The metaphors that are used to describe those quests have iconic qualities. They symbolize order, control, regularity, and a sense of timeless certainty; in sum, they are expressions of power—the panacea of anxiety.

The quest for security is recounted also in the stories of a common search. In times less equivocally theocentric than our own, the quest was for a Via Illuminata. Hopefully, it would lead to a miraculous experience similar to the one on the road to Damascus. It might be barred by the ordeals of a ritualistic hegira to Medina following the path of the Prophet. It could be heard in the epiphanies of those cenobitic communities founded by the Covenanters of Quram. It could be witnessed in the ecstatic experience of sensory deprivation sought by the anchorites isolated in the desert wastes of Scete.

Then, too, in response to an exhortation, echoing the one voiced by Peter of Amiens, surnamed the Hermit, one could vouchsafe his security by the route of a more active quest. He was urged to become a crusader in a Holy War waged against infidels, a war waged to yoke all secular and ecclesiastical power in an oxymoronic hegemony that prescribed death to the nonbeliever and thus hoped to secure peace on earth for all men.

The political echoes of such questing chiliasm continually reverberate throughout the corridors of history. The pre-Christian *polis* of Plato's Republic shared an Aryan legacy with oriental versions of the same Promethean myths. There followed in our era the Judaeo-Christian *kerygma*—the final judgment and salvation for believers in the Kingdom of God. Later there were post-Christian fantasies, such worldly variations of the same political theme as Thomas More's Utopia and Francis Bacon's New Atlantis. These are the better known of a welter of mythical and millenarian worlds. They planned and promised political as well as economic, religious, and personal security in the now and the hereafter. The prospective members were an

[2] Stanley E. Hyman, *The Tangled Bank: Darwin, Marx, Frazer and Freud as Imaginative Writers* (New York: Atheneum, 1962).

elect group whose price of membership was total surrender, a submersion of personal self in an autocratic community of believers.

The eighteenth and nineteenth centuries witnessed the beginning of a progressive shift to a man-centered, nationalistic ideology. Men, as self-consciously rational creatures, were held to be masters of their fate, freely able to select their choice from among thoughtfully weighted alternatives.[3] We too in our times subscribe to a man-centered security. We locate its power and primary responsibility in political space. We try to protect it from outside encroachment by physical, moral, economic, political, and even social boundaries that insulate by isolation from destructive foreign contact. We have used the natural barriers of geography to encourage parochial ties of kinship. We strengthen these bonds of proximity and familiarity with the valences of social custom and the affect of taboo. The formal values which these relationships establish define the nature and limits of allegiance to local, regional, national, and international alliances. Thereby security acquires its many political dimensions that are construed as synonymous with such group concepts as religion, government, sovereign integrity, loyalty, freedom, and independence.

The twentieth century ushered in the era of psychological man. A focus of the search for security for the first time turned to forces wholly centered within man and their reflections mirrored in his relations with fellow men. These expressions and reflections have been used to explain the similarities of thought, feeling, and behavior among men of like mind—men who have been similarly reared and therefore share the same values. As for the shaping role of transcendental influence, Gerald Heard has summarized the currently held majority opinion of the psychological nature of man in the observation: "Newton banished God from nature, Darwin banished Him from life, Freud drove Him from the last fastness, the soul. It was all latent in Newton, in Descartes, in Galileo: mechanism

[3] H. Stuart Hughes, *Consciousness and Society* (New York: Knopf, 1958).

would conquer all, once it had conquered nature, for man's body was sprung from nature and his mind from his body."[4]

Freud, a nineteenth-century man whose formulations of man's dreams, anxieties, and capacities have indelibly marked the twentieth century, saw the quest for security as a foredoomed flight into neuroticism when he wrote: "Life as we find it is too hard for us; it entails too much pain, too many disappointments, impossible tasks. In order to bear it, we cannot do without palliative measures. We cannot do without auxiliary constructions as Theodor Fontane tells us. There are perhaps three such measures: powerful deflections which cause us to make light of our misery; substitutive satisfactions which diminish it; and intoxicating substances, which make us insensitive to it. Something of this kind is indispensable."[5]

Shadowed by this darkened light Freud explicated the nature of man's anxiety and his bumbling efforts to assuage it. His version of this odyssey is another in a long line of old philosophers' tales that describe man's path hewn out of the dark wood of insecurity. As Fromm says: "By devoting his interests to the phenomena of individual emotional and mental disturbances, he [Freud] led us to the top of the volcano and made us look into the boiling crater."[6] The Dantean quality of this and other neopsychoanalytic writing is taken by some as an act of *lèse majesté*, for, as they see it, these searchers have dethroned the old gods without altering the need for them or providing the means to do without them. In the stead of the god of the Via Illuminata, they have ensconced a secular facsimile fashioned in the image of science.

The choice of metaphors suggests that a common imagery shared by all those who describe man's quest for security implies a common need to escape from a common fear. The destructive forces each sees in the boiling crater are the same

[4] Gerald Heard, *The Third Morality* (New York: Morrow, 1937).

[5] Sigmund Freud, "Civilization and Its Discontents," *Standard Edition of the Complete Psychological Works*, XXI, 75.

[6] Erich Fromm, *Escape from Freedom* (New York: Farrar and Rinehart, 1961), p. 9.

ones ascribed to the Devil by the medieval past. They were transmogrified into the blind instinctual forces of a self-evolving nature by the demythologizing, secular transformations of the nineteenth century. *Autre temps, autre mœurs*—imagery also has a time-base in style and fashion. The gamut man has run from animism to pantheism to monotheism to scientism has in common above all else the urgent necessity for an imagery of security.

Darwin's formulations of the struggle for existence gave a new symbolic form of biological substance to the metaphysical notions of destructive insecurity when he equated it with the forces of nature and described them as red in tooth and claw. Freud added a psychological dimension to the same forces. As he formulated the instincts and their vicissitudes, even love, which earlier times saw as transcendentally inspired, is initially an entirely self-satisfying, biological security-move; narcissistic, he called it. Love can be freed from hate, its destructive partner in ambivalence, only as a consequence of a slowly acquired maturation. Even then, it is subject to the relapse of regression.

Freud's is an epigenetic model of man's psychic growth. It is a development in a social milieu which supplies both the *vis a tergo* and the *vis a fronte*. It is a model formed from component elements that develop as a consequence of the cued interaction of environmental influences and genotypic potentialities. The biological limitations of human infancy impose a necessity for total dependence upon a succoring environment. The child's perceptual capacities are organized by it. In turn, the environment orchestrates the burgeoning of behavior, affect, cognition, and social values. Accordingly, environment becomes the shaping influence in the formation of personality and character. In gross and subtle ways, it fashions morals and ethics.

The Freudian theory of personality development roots the ultimate in security in an archetypal oceanic unity. This figure of speech describes a time and the blissful state in which the *anlage* of self and its totally providing, nourishing mother were indissociably linked in symbiosis. In that dimensionless beginning, whim was anticipated and commanded response without need for prior stimulus. Again, the evocative metaphors that describe the undisturbed serenity of that state use the same paradisical allusions that have been used by the oriental and western mystics in their descriptions of the enlightenment of *satori* and the miraculous transfiguration that leads to the beatific vision.

It is also explicit that the cost of such out-of-the-world tranquility is the complete loss of one's persona. Self must totally surrender to other to achieve that state of security. Only when the worldly boundaries that define objects disappear in the envelope of an embracing union can the self and the other merge in perfect security. It is then that the fabled triad of wholeness, harmony, and radiance reigns supreme. It is from this sensory experience of bliss that the traditional literature of love and religion draw their similar vocabularies. Romantic love and religion are the social institutions par excellence that share in the joint responsibility of assuaging man's anxiety. Indeed, many have observed that man is the social animal that many since Aristotle have recognized him to be because it is only in the presence of fellow men who, sharing the same needs and values, have their common experience of dread muted. Likewise, the genesis of man's talent for fashioning culture has been traced to this organizing principle.

Society is molded by these forces. In turn, it becomes the instrument for the achievement of these values. Stabilized in this manner, it can protect, defend, and provide, and by so doing, it can augment and perpetuate the security furnished originally by the members of one's family. Society's role is preformed in the mold of one's biological family. Ties of kinship, legal as well as biological, confer upon men the status of brothers. Matrilocal and patrilocal territories literally become "motherland" and "fatherland" in language of society.

Political man bears the social stamp of his family's rearing patterns. These fit the young to the mirrored expectations of their elders and thereby achieve what Thomas More described as the "beste state of a Publiyque Weale." The issue of what is best is another of the many moot points of value. Investigations in recent times have produced a rich but again a bewilderingly varied and uneven assortment of conclusions about the nature of man. Nevertheless, a few salient features of the security quests of modern man do stand out.

The political socialization that prepares one to participate collectively in security maneuvers is a learned process. It is most influenced by the same agents and forces that influence all other behavior. It is essentially conservative, designed to maintain the status quo. It does this through the binding, unifying process of love.

Men are bound together by affective valences; these are molded by the love they have for each other. They love the system into which they are born—their family and its social surrogates. But the quality of love and its derivatives is often strained as it is transmitted by the hierarchy of persons to whom one looks for expressions of it. This hierarchy structures emotional distance. The ties it establishes among people are themselves a function of the manner in which they were reared.

The affective experience of childhood ordinarily is a consequence of close proximity and responsive physical contacts. This is illustrated by Harlow's experiments with laboratory monkeys.[7] They make it clear that responsive contact is an indispensable prerequisite for all of the subsequent transactions of life. Similarly, the investigations by Spitz,[8] Bowlby,[9] and others of the consequence of early maternal deprivation bear out these conclusions: the qualities that are transmitted to successive generations are derivatives of the positive tangible expressions of love. All subsequent relationships are cast in symbolic variations of this mold. Erickson's inquiries into the developmental epochs of life suggest that all moral, ideological, and ethical propensities depend on the ratio of basic trust and

[7] Harry Harlow, "The Nature of Love," *American Psychologist*, XIII (1958), 673–685.

[8] R. A. Spitz, "The Role of Ecological Factors in Emotional Development in Infancy," *Child Development*, XX (1949), 145–155.

[9] John Bowlby, "Separation Anxiety: A Critical Review of the Literature," *Journal of Child Psychology and Psychiatry*, I (1960), 251–269.

mistrust that emerges as hope as the newborn child reaches out to its caretakers and as they bring it the response of mutuality.[10] Indeed, there are profound physical effects that are the consequence of an absence of this vital exchange. Spitz found that of ninety-one infants raised in a foundling home without mothers, over one-third died. All but a couple in his words "became human wrecks who behaved either in the manner of agitated or of apathetic idiots."[11]

There are data to show that the skewing of less dramatic social expressions is also a correlate of the sociological and psychological tides in the human ecosystem. Metroux and Mead describe the child-rearing practices of overprotection among the French that they contend result in political distrust and disaffection.[12] Pinner's studies of Belgian, Dutch, and French students elaborate on these suggestions to show that those family practices that make the world outside the family appear hostile and treacherous result in a distrust of political institutions and a set of political beliefs characterized by low esteem, opposition to authority, and negative feelings about government in general.[13] Wylie's observations of French children in the Vaucluse substantiate the impression that cynical attitudes toward politics and public officials are derivatives of their adults' constant reference to government as a source of evil and the men who run it as instruments of evil.[14] Pye's studies of the Burmese[15] as well as Adorno's studies of

[10] Erik H. Erikson, "Identity and the Life Cycle," Selected Papers, Monograph I, *Psychological Issues* (New York: International Universities Press, 1959), pp. 18–171.

[11] Spitz, "The Role of Ecological Factors."

[12] R. Metroux and M. Mead, *Themes in French Culture* (Stanford, Calif.: Stanford University Press, 1954), pp. 16, 27–35.

[13] F. A. Pinner, "Parental Over-Protection and Political Distrust," *Annals of the American Academy of Political and Social Science*, CCCLXI (1965), 58–70.

[14] Lawrence Wylie, *Village in the Vaucluse* (Cambridge, Mass.: Harvard University Press, 1951), p. 208.

[15] L. W. Pye, *Politics, Personality and Nation-Building* (New Haven: Yale University Press, 1962), pp. 182–183.

American college students[16] underscore the same general findings: homes that fail to provide youth with the atmosphere and opportunity to develop democratic cooperative skills tend to produce more instances of American youth with fascistic tendencies on the one hand and of Burmese youth suspicious of strangers on the other.

The metaphysical state conceived as the paradigm of security is one in which both man's and nature's destructive forces are mastered. The moral control necessary for man to accomplish his part has been variously attributed. The hard, painful, disappointing life which Freud lamented derives in no small measure from the pricks and bites of conscience. The litany of these "oughts" and "musts" that curb spontaneous expression owes its sanctions to both implicit and explicit threats of punishment—the levy of violence. The anxiety threats provoke anticipates a loss of self. This is the antithesis of union, wholeness, and security; it comes in many forms: shame is a frequent one appearing as the reflected belittlement of an established guilt; a loss of self-esteem is the consequence of derogation rendered as a concluded judgment. Other cognate forms include ostracism, disenfranchisement, and, of course, physical injury. In addition to all else, these are quite painful separations, for in a very literal sense they are the epitome of an invidious comparison with others. And, of course, there is death itself that lies at the core of all these symbolic cognates; it is the act of irremediable exclusion.[17]

The awe and terror that the emptiness of such threatened dissolution provokes vests all symbols and agencies of power with an aura of violence. In the young child it instills what Piaget has described as a heteronomous morality, that is, a respect for authority that regards adult rules as sacred and unchangeable. For the unquestioning child, the attributes of

[16] T. W. Adorno *et al.*, *The Authoritarian Personality* (New York: Harper and Brothers, 1950).

[17] Norman O. Brown, "Death, Time and Eternity," in *Life Against Death: The Psychoanalytical Meaning of History* (Middletown, Conn.: Wesleyan University Press, 1959), pp. 87–109.

omnipotence and omniscience become the hallmarks of an absolute authority that is literally the author of life and death.[18]

Symbolic transformation and mythopoeic displacement then permit these impressive experiences of childhood to be generalized. They then become the cultural forms which Cassirer believes are interpretations of reality. Bidney suggests that myth originates wherever thought and imagination are employed initially or are deliberately used to promote social delusions. In prescientific cultures, mythic symbolism endowed the source of power with a life-giving and a life-taking potential. Kings and gods, therefore, were adorned with the trappings of absolutism. Their faithful followers, subjects and disciples, all those whose adherence earned them the favor of the omnipotent, become an elect—a chosen people. The elect of the omnipotent govern by a ritualized right that legitimates their superordinate status by the charisma of divine authority. They are anointed thereby and by this ritual incorporate within their person the earthly counterpart of moral and ethical power.

Mumford believes that it was by the command authority of royalty that the control of power latent in huge human-labor machines was organized, concentrated, and directed.[19] The energy of these machines, comprised of thousands of replaceable human parts, was used to build the first cities as tributes to the gods and the sovereigns who, in the dynasties of the Pharaohs, were one and the same, immortalized as king-gods. The power inherent in such energy machines was epitomized in the person of the king. He was the tangible symbol of majesty. His court, his palace, his capitol, his nation personified his power.[20]

Power of this kind and magnitude is easily reified. Thus objectified, it acquires charismatic qualities which have the additional property of extension to other objects. By the processes of communion, ordination, and ennoblement, persons

[18] J. H. Flavell, *The Developmental Psychologies of Jean Piaget* (Princeton, N.J.: D. Van Nostrand, 1963), pp. 290–297.

[19] Lewis Mumford, "Utopia, the City and the Machine," *Daedalus*, XCIV (1965), 271–292.

[20] Henri Frankfort, *Kingship and the Gods* (Chicago: University of Chicago Press, 1948).

as well as things are invested with influence and thereby power is replicated. This process of symbolic investiture endows the symbols of crown, scepter, seal, miter, gavel, and title with an aura of transferred potency. In other social dimensions, a similar process occurs in which power is symbolically communicated to surrogates. The honorific title of father is bestowed figuratively upon persons who stand in this line of succession. The faithful become "children" and peers become "brothers" by this token.

Over the centuries, this transferred vitality has led to successive generations of social institutions each endowed with supportive and palliative functions akin to the protections of individual psychological defenses of which they are homologues. Society then, in sociological space like the city in geographic space, mirrors man's psychological space in its ramified designs for security. It has evolved its present form from the same kind of trial-and-error empiricism which has led to the natural selection of certain biological traits. They are developmentally adapted to ensure physical survival in a potentially lethal environment. In a complementary manner, social man has evolved an array of palliative substitutes and displacement activities with which to cope with that quiet desperation which Thoreau said lies at the heart of all men.

Primarily these palliatives are means to contain, refute, or convert the death-potential man has learned to recognize within himself and in the environment around him. For most men, death stalks in the natural forms of the hard life of which Freud wrote: "But in every human ideology and in the experience of every human individual, death is the great adversary."[21]

More of the world now enjoys more affluence than has ever been true in the past. This is not to say that there are not large areas of unshriven blight and abysmal poverty or large blocs of persons whose wretched standard of living converts every concern with security to a desperate search for food and shelter and the barest means of survival. Rather, it is that the state of

[21] Sigmund Freud, "Beyond the Pleasure Principle," *Standard Edition of the Complete Psychological Works*, XVIII, 7–64.

relative affluence for a sizable portion of the world has reached a point at which, all other things being equal, the population will double in the next twenty-eight years. This is a direct index of affluence, for this rate of survival and growth is attributable not only to a high birth rate (more than 30 per 1,000 population per year in the less well developed countries) but also to a rapid decline in the death rate that accompanies economic development and improved health and sanitary conditions. The point here considered is that affluence is also accompanied by such security problems as are posed by overcrowding, accelerated mobility, and a myriad of related psychosocial problems.

There is the paradoxical phenomenon of affording discontent, that is, being sufficiently free from the stultifying harassments of physical existence to be able to invidiously contrast one's state with that of others. The anxiety and dissatisfaction which are provoked by such a discovery suggest and encourage the use of power. There are ample historical data testifying to the use of force to remedy the discontent of groups and nations who have seen their have-not status in a disadvantaged light in contrast with what others have. The probability of translating discontent into action—war and other violence—as well as the manner of its display by individuals and groups, large and small, has intrigued the inquiries of clinicians and the studies of behavioral scientists concerned with the ways and means for the resolution of conflict.

There are data that strongly suggest that the choice is the complex function of an ideological matrix. Generally speaking, a predisposition to the use of power rather than use of the alternative strategy of a peaceful solution depends on the prevailing influence of social values, principles of ethics, and moral deterrents that are acquired as incidental learning during the process of maturation.

Ziblatt makes the point that Americans place a peculiar emphasis on individual responsibility.[22] In a comment on the

[22] David Ziblatt, "High School Extra-Curricular Activities and Political Socialization," *Annals of the American Academy of Political and Social Science*, CCCLXI (1965), 20–31.

world-wide reaction to the violence explicit in the Kennedy assassination, one observer has noted that whereas Europeans invent conspiracies to take responsibility for social events, Americans invent individuals. Robert Lane's study of political ideology found that working-class men, rather than feel powerless, believe that anyone could become more powerful if he wanted to badly enough, "just as anyone who wanted to and had the skills and got the breaks could be rich." Lane epitomizes their beliefs as follows: "Power is dependent upon organization and effort . . . the decision is your own. . . . If one has little power at any given time, it is his own fault for failing to organize his interests."[23]

A recent review of a symposium on the natural history of aggression makes the point that "human aggression in particular has become too serious a subject to leave to the humanists."[24] It harks back to an observation made by Hobbes in 1651: "As the nature of Foule weather lyeth not in a showre or two of rain; but in an inclination thereto of many dayes together; so the nature of War, consisteth not in actuall fighting; but in the known disposition thereto, during all the time there is no assurance to the contrary."

A generation ago in a well known exchange of letters between Einstein and Freud, Freud wrote that the kernel of the matter of controlling violence was "the transfer of power to a larger combination, founded on the community of sentiments linking up its members." "All the rest," he went on to say, "is mere tautology and glosses." He observed that while he saw little likelihood of being able to suppress humanity's aggressive tendencies, "whatever makes for cultural development is working also against war."[25]

Since the time of that exchange, there has been a series of wars, both large and small, world-wide as well as limited in

[23] Robert Lane, *Political Ideology* (Glencoe, Ill.: Free Press, 1962), p. 172.
[24] "Man and Beast," *Times Literary Supplement*, September 23, 1965, pp. 817–818.
[25] *A Correspondence Between Albert Einstein and Sigmund Freud*, trans. Gilbert Stuart (London: Peace Pledge Union, 1939).

scope. A transfer of power to a larger combination on an international scale has been tried for the second time. In certain respects, the United Nations has been successful in bringing some expressions of open violence under control by its display of collective strength. In each successful instance, however, the display of power has had to be backed by the potential if not the actual presence of physical force. Moral suasion and other power displays that lack the dimension of force manifestly have been less successful. And yet there is reason to hope that one need not accept resignedly the inevitability of war as the only available solution for international problems of security.

The use of what the late Dag Hammarskjold called preventive diplomacy has been the mainstay of our slow evolution to a peaceful coexistence. He saw preventive diplomacy, which Arthur Larson sees as old-fashioned power politics, as a short-term tactic useful in dealing with situations that are either the result of or imply risks for the creation of a power vacuum between the main contending blocs.[26]

At a practical level, then, peace-keeping has been a holding operation which hopes only to gain time for undertaking diplomatic negotiations. This is a long-used tactic which attempts to employ in the group situation the delaying device of a cooling-off period. It provides a respite of demonstrated worth in the individual instance.

The characteristic of socialized man is his acceptance of the principle of a division of labor as a guide for his life. Operationally this means that he accepts the fact that he is part of a system in which duties and responsibilities are variously allocated so that a maximal advantage for all can be had from encouraging a focused attention to the development of special competency of each part of the system.

The evolution of modern industrial society is witness to the efficiency of this principle of diversification. Efficiency is accomplished as a consequence of the distribution of responsi-

[26] Dag Hammerskjold, *International Conciliation*, No. 554, September 1965, p. 12.

bility for various degrees of operational decisions. The technological revolution promised by the wider use of automation techniques depends on the demonstrated utility of the same principle. The operational pattern that results is a matrix of branches, each linked by a nodal point at which decisions are made. The selection of the optimal route through the decision tree is the cumulative function of the choice that is made at each juncture.

This is an example of art copying nature inasmuch as the basic model from which this is drawn is the biological one. The special function of learning that begins with the raw data of primitive, undifferentiated response to provocative stimulus is a slowly evolved process in which a successful outcome at one time maximizes the likelihood of a repeated performance the next time guided by the expectation of a similar reward. Random trial and error is gradually converted into a goal-directed activity as a result of modulation by the frequency of off- and on-target responses that scores hits and misses or successes and failures or rewards and punishments. In this fashion, the organism—or its responding part—modifies its character, the time, direction, and even the nature of its response so as to attune it more perfectly to the environment.

The physiological, psychological, and sociological details of this process of acquisition in a gross manner at least have been alluded to. What is important is that there is a different time-base required for adaptation at each level of the system. At the molecular level in single organisms, genetic mutations bring about modifications in structure that have short- and far-reaching consequences immediately or years later. At the cellular, organ, and body system levels, similar kinds of unique changes occur, with the net result that each organism not only bears an environmental imprint superimposed on its personal history, but also is the legatee of the similar experience of its antecedents.

In a fleeting way, then, one sees how social and psychological influences are converted and transmuted with the same evolutionary consequences. The rate at which modification and adaptation occur varies enormously—too slow for some, too rapid for others.

Man the maker—the *homo faber* of the philosophers—is an impatient creature whose discontent with the stochastic operations of evolution has caused him to tinker with the spontaneous order that has regulated his life up to now. While his success in the control of some of his physical environments has been considerable, his failure to match this performance in the environment of value is the cause of dismay and the basis of forebodings.[27]

The quest for security in the world of reality, then, becomes an endless pursuit in which what is alleged to be the goal in fact becomes the choice of means.

[27] A. and L. Weinberg (eds.), *Instead of Violence: Writings by the Great Advocates of Peace and Non-Violence Throughout History* (Boston: Beacon Press, 1963).

Comment by ROBERT J. STEIN, M.D.

Dr. Rome has given us the opportunity to understand the broad and generalized concepts of man's quest for security from early times and has described in detail the more specific psychological, both personal and social, concepts of this eternal struggle. To understand the clear meaning of Dr. Rome's erudite discussion, I found it important to separate the two words of the title of this symposium, that is, "quest" and "security." In the broader sense, Dr. Rome appears to define security as a metaphysical state and beautifully illustrates this concept by describing the emotional reactions of the visionaries and mystics and various religious promises of security. In this sense, quest for security is seen as dreams, either fantasy- or reality-based. At the same time, Dr. Rome defines security more specifically by suggesting that anxiety can be allayed through controlled regularity or, actually, a sense of timeless certainty. Maybe reality is more uncertainty or relative certainty rather than timeless certainty, and absolute or timeless certainty might be fantasy. Maybe, therefore, the most important word of the title is "quest" rather than "security." Dr. Rome has vividly shown us the history of this quest from primitive times, and this quest should continue as long as security remains relative.

The most stimulating part of Dr. Rome's paper, from a psychiatric standpoint, was his showing us the evolution of psychological man through many peepholes. We all know the deepest convictions of man are determined by emotional rather than logical processes. The search for security is revealed by man's reactions and interpersonal relationships, stemming from self-concept or self-realization and his adjustment within families, social organizations, political institutions, and beliefs. In other words, the quest for emotional security includes the seeking of security in effectual relations with others and in organizing one's capacities to meet the demands in life. Emotional security draws its roots in part from the satisfaction of quest for power and in part from pleasure (which the Freudians regard as sexual). We all are aware of the pleasure derived from emotionally satisfactory interpersonal relationships which at least have the potentiality of becoming sexualized. The Adlerian concept of compensatory striving toward superiority has much in common with the concept of striving toward emotional security. In Freudian theory, the sexual drive and aspirations are conceived in the broadest possible terms, going far beyond the physiologic, including elements similar to those in striving toward emotional security and those emphasized by the Adlerians. In successful sexual expression, security and power are but two slightly different aspects of the same unity of experience.

Dr. Rome, in a choice of metaphors, suggests that the common imagery shared by all those who write of man's quest for security implies a common need to escape from a common fear. I believe we should also be aware of the variations in the concepts of security which individuals may have even though they are from like cultures. We all know that security or freedom from anxiety for one person does not necessarily mean the same for another. This again re-emphasizes the concept that there is no such thing as an absolute or complete security and that this term should be defined only in the relative sense. It is my belief that in attempting to make our concept of security absolute so that we are free from anxiety, we may, in the long run, only be creating more anxieties. This is best illustrated by the present-day social, economic, and political concept of governments to provide security to the individual "from the womb to the tomb." The government has become more and more a father image. He assures the individual that he will not only take care of his physical needs but provide security from all worries and emotional problems. The individual cannot help becoming less secure as he becomes more dependent on this father image. Perhaps this is what Dr. Rome was telling us when he mentions surrendering of the personal self to the social self. Maybe our quest or goal should be to learn to tolerate better our anxieties or insecurities. In any case, with vague and imperfect insight into the truth, maybe we have taken too much refuge in words. It seems fitting, therefore, to conclude with the memorable last request of Goethe, "More light."

Comment by MERRILL T. EATON, M.D.

Of the dangers to man Dr. Rome emphasizes war as a major threat to human safety. Reasoning that the behavior of a society is determined by the attitudes of the individuals composing it, he finds the basic cause of war to be individual human aggression. He points out that the tendency to use force or violence in reaction to discontent rather than applying some other coping method is dependent upon social values which have been learned in childhood.

Two solutions are suggested. Somewhat pessimistically, the idea that violence might be suppressed or controlled by the transfer of power to larger combinations is presented. A universal state, a "parliament of man," a successful United Nations might abolish war. More enthusiasm is expressed for the possibility of reducing, rather than merely controlling, aggressive tendencies through the application of psychological insights to child-rearing. If children develop self-respect, learn to love rather than to hate, to trust rather than to suspect, a better and greater society may evolve.

Obviously the two solutions must be sought simultaneously. Making our own society one of individuals unlikely to resort to violence does not automatically make potential predators nonviolent, though we must concede that in time kindness may win over an enemy and love disarm an aggressor. In the meantime, while we negotiate and throughout efforts to tame the predators, we must protect ourselves.

This is true on the local as well as the international level. If our children are taught to love, they must be protected from exploitation. If they are taught to trust, they must be safe from betrayal. If one is to play after dark in Central Park, talk without concern to the stranger, and open the door to whoever knocks, the policeman must be nearby. This is not to suggest that if others fail to strive for peace, their failure justifies our neglecting efforts to reduce our own aggressions.

Surely we can build a better, a safer, society if we help children grow up as free from anxiety and as disinclined to use violence as possible. Education of parents and teachers, efforts to combat poverty and overcrowding, and community mental health programs can contribute to this.

However, before we can achieve optimum success in reducing harmful aggression, some very basic research into the nature of aggressiveness is necessary. Is aggression biologically or culturally determined? Throughout history, human beings have fought as individuals and in groups. Is fighting as natural a part of being human as is eating and reproducing? Or is fighting solely a reaction to frustration; a maladaptive, acquired, learned way of coping with anxiety? To the extent that aggression is a product of frustration it should be relatively easy to eliminate.

Even if aggression is a fundamental part of being human, it can be controlled. After all, society controls other basic drives. Our eating habits, and, to a degree, our sex habits are not those of primitive man. However, simple suppression of an instinctual drive is not effective; it gives rise to symptoms, and at times the inhibitions give way and neurotic conflict is acted out. A basic drive can be directed into constructive, or at least safe, activities.

Is love and trust enough, or does man *need* an outlet for his aggression?

A Political Scientist's View

HAROLD W. STOKE

President of Queens College from 1958 until his retirement in 1965, HAROLD W. STOKE early in his distinguished career as an educator and author taught political science at the University of Nebraska (1930–1937). Subsequently he served as president of the University of New Hampshire (1944–1947) and of Louisiana State University (1947–1951), as dean of the Graduate School at the University of Washington (1951–1955), and as dean of the Graduate School of Arts and Sciences at New York University (1955–1958). From 1949 to 1951 he was on the board of directors of the Oak Ridge Institution of Nuclear Studies. Dr. Stoke is a member of the American Academy of Arts and Sciences and a former president of the American Association of Graduate Schools (1955–1956). His most recent book is *The American College President* (1959).

JASPER B. SHANNON, who is a professor of political science at the University of Nebraska, is the author of *Money and Politics* (1959). W. ROBERT PARKS is the president of Iowa State University; his study *Soil Conservation Districts in Action* was published in 1952.

From the discussions of this subject which have already been presented it is clear that men find a sense of security in a thousand forms. I suggest, however, that the quest for security grows out of a single source—fear. We seek to protect ourselves from what we fear most. Whether it is violence, loneliness, discomfort, illness, or the hereafter, for each fear we try to build a bulwark of protection—personal or institutional.

Two centuries ago Samuel Johnson wrote:

> How small of all that human hearts endure,
> That part which laws or kings can cause or cure.

There is still much that human hearts endure about which governments can do little, but the areas in which governments are active are no longer small. The great hazards of life against which men universally have always sought protection have become concerns of government almost everywhere. Those hazards are, as they have always been, the fears of violence, of hunger, of helplessness arising from accident, illness, and old age. Where once the quest for security was a highly individual one, today it has become collective. The American term "social security" is both useful and accurate.

What happened to place government so near the center of the modern quest for security is a direct consequence of a titanic industrial and scientific revolution which is still gathering force. This revolution has vastly increased the capacity to provide security, and simultaneously, it has brought about the readjustment or reorganization of virtually every social, political, and economic institution under which men live. It is a revolution so vast and fundamental that it not only alters every physical phase of life, but draws into its vortex our intellectual and philosophical conceptions as well. We not only live differently, we think and feel differently from any previous generation. We have grafted upon our inheritance from the industrial revolution the immensely greater power of modern science—physics, chemistry, biology, and mathematics—with consequences which our slower processes of social invention find almost unmanageable.

Our new powers have solved some of our old problems. We can, for example, now win most of our battles with Nature in the production and preservation of food. The great plagues, which used to scourge whole populations, have been brought under control. Years have been added to the average span of life, and infant mortality has been so reduced that population increases are staggering. We can now provide ourselves with more goods, services, and comforts with less labor than we previously dreamed possible. But our exhilaration at these achievements is tempered by the bewildering adjustments they have forced upon our institutions, our ideas, and even our personal lives.

Most of these readjustments focus on the changed relationship of the individual to his employment and to the community of which he is now a part. Where once the means by which to attain such security as he had were in his own hands, now these means are a part of a huge and intricate organization of which he is a member, but which, as an individual, he cannot control. If one still wished to live by candlelight, one might even now continue to make his own candles, but if one wants electric light, one must join the complex technical, financial, and political organization which alone can produce high-voltage lines. One may still take elementary steps to look after one's own health, but if one wants to escape smallpox or cholera, one must become subject to a scientific and social organization required to produce effective vaccinations.

The same forces of modern life have transformed the means by which people make a living, whether in advanced or in backward countries. The Japanese farmer growing a few mulberry trees to feed silkworms may never have heard of Dupont, but his trees were as effectively destroyed by nylon as if vandals had cut them down. The camel caravans of the deserts disappear when the helicopters and caterpillar tractors come. The gondoliers of Venice are displaced by motorboats and their songs by tape recordings. From what can be summarily described as the forces of modernization there is no place to hide.

The consequences of this loosening of the individual's control over his own security can be seen more clearly than anywhere else in the modern phenomenon of urbanization. All of the benefits of industrialization, of mass communication, mass transportation, of services and conveniences are now most sharply focused in the cities, and all the attendant problems as well. Cities are a product of the combined forces of modernization and consequently are becoming everywhere the same. Throughout the world, from Johannesburg to Rio, every large city begins to look like New York. Cities force people into a mutual dependence in which each person achieves his own security by contributing to a collective security in which he shares but which he could not possibly produce for himself. This is why, even in countries with huge unoccupied areas, as, for example, in Mexico, the drainage of rural populations into cities goes on, and in crowded countries the urban areas grow even more crowded.

One of every eight Japanese lives in Tokyo; a quarter of all the people of Great Britain live within twenty-five miles of the center of London, and in the United States, twenty-five million people live within fifty miles of the Empire State building.

The consequences are awesome. Every day all of these people must be fed. Every day most of them must work in order to ensure the flow of income which in turn must be exchanged for the goods and services which each produces and each requires. Every day millions must be transported. They must all have places to sleep. They must have entertainment, education, water, electricity, sanitation, police and fire protection. These are stern necessities. Interruption for only a few hours can result in inconvenience, panic, and even death. Yet the vast majority of these individuals produce not an ounce of the food they eat; as individuals they do not own the means by which they make a living; they cannot command their own transportation. If water, light, or telephones fail, the few hundreds or thousands of people with the know-how to restore such services become the few on whom the many depend. In short, as a part of his increased security and his greater well-being, modern man has become a part of a network of public and private organizations forming a complex pattern of authority, technical skills, finance, investment, planning, and discipline. If he wants what this organization can provide him, he must become a dues-paying member with all the rights, privileges, and obligations.

It is not strange, under these conditions of intense specialization and mutual dependence, that we should turn to government as the most appropriate supervisor or trustee of these new instruments of security. The reasons are self-evident. The basic responsibility of government for the protection of life and property, its tradition of authority, its universal relationship to all its citizens, make it a more logical depository of a common interest than any other institution. It is, therefore, fair to ask how effective governments themselves are proving as supervisors or trustees of these new capacities which modern knowledge has created.

Measured by this test of effectiveness, the governments of the world, by and large, may be ranged along a spectrum with great concentrations at the two extremes. At one extreme are those governments which feel the impact of technological developments, but which are too weak or unstable to manage them effectively. The great majority of governments in Asia, Africa, and South America, and even some in Europe, fall in this category. At the other extreme are the Communist countries which have seized outright the means by which security can be achieved and have transferred to the governments the total responsibility for providing individual security. The governments in these two extreme groups comprehend most of the populations of the world. Between them a few governments, the United States and some of the European countries, are distributed near a midpoint between socialism and individualism. There are, of course, many variations and degrees in the classification of governments as weak or strong, but here we are concerned with only one major test: how much have they helped or hindered their people in their quest for security against their age-old and universal hazards?

If we examine what, for this purpose, have been called "weak" governments, they are universally characterized by a lack of confidence on the part of those who live under them or on the part of other peoples who deal with them. This lack of confidence shows itself in many forms. It shows itself in doubt as to a government's stability and continuity, in the reliability of its contracts, in its ability to maintain law and order, in its due process of law. Under such governments people are thrown back upon their own ingenuity and resources. In any crisis their first impulse is not toward an expectation of government protection, but toward self-preservation. There is always a temptation to take law into their own hands. Politics is usually violent and intense; seldom is the transfer of power peaceful. Secrecy and intrigue flourish as normal and expected operations. Tax evasion is rampant, for there is little sense of moral obligation on the part of citizens to support governments which provide so little and demand so much.

In these weak governments the raw struggle of life is ameliorated scarcely at all by any sense of community. Where it is every citizen for himself, some succeed better than others and those who do succeed develop little sympathy for those who do not. Hence the puzzling phenomenon: the tremendous extremes of wealth and poverty which in so many countries exist side by side. This is why billions of dollars poured into some countries as foreign aid or even as investment have had only a trifling effect upon the general level of well-being. Under weak governments men work out channels of power and self-protection outside of government—channels in which they have more confidence—family ties, social and economic classes, labor unions, voluntary organizations, and even fraternal orders. An overriding loyalty to a weak and unstable political regime is a luxury few can afford.

Perhaps the inability of weak governments to handle the complexities of modern life is best seen in what happens to their money. Money has become an increasingly important component of every modern economy. Unfortunately, among weak governments, money which is stable and exchangeable is rare. Suppose, for example, you visited any country of North Africa —Morocco, Algeria, Egypt. A familiar sight would be that of an Arabian man riding a burro while his veiled and robed wife strode behind. Some breeze might disturb her veil and she reaches up hastily to secure it, but in her movement you might have caught a flash of a bare arm, with possibly a number of bracelets, silver, perhaps gold. Such a display seems surprising, but what you have had is a quick and unintended look into the family vault. You have had a short course on the country's economy—the nature, value, and safekeeping of wealth. You have learned that the only wealth to be trusted is silver and gold —not the coinage of the realm and certainly not its paper money. If one must accept money, it is desirable to exchange it as quickly as possible, preferably into a more stable, although forbidden, foreign money. Trust no bank—its contents are too easily withheld. Buried treasure is not safe from marauders, hence in a number of countries, given these and other conditions, the safest place for wealth is to attach it to the person of one's wife so that even she cannot remove it. It is an extreme illustration, but only in degree. Why in so many countries is paper money printed in denominations as small as $2\frac{1}{2}$¢? Because all but the most worthless coins tend to disappear. (Before we leave the Arab, however, we should credit him with a definite advantage over so-called advanced systems—he can take an inventory of his wealth at any time and even count his money in the dark!)

Under such monetary systems, the recourse of the poor is barter and the black market. The rich buy land, hoard silver and gold, and establish numbered bank accounts in Switzerland and Lebanon. It is unnecessary to ask why it is so difficult in many countries to induce foreign or domestic investments in private enterprises, in roads, schools, factories, and public institutions, why interest rates are so high, why wealth is concealed.

Nevertheless, there is, paradoxically, scarcely a government so weak or a country so poor but that one finds the presence there of evidence of the modern industrial world—public utilities, electricity, the ubiquitous automobile with its social benefits and strains. As frequently as not this phenomenon is traceable not to the capacity of the local domestic government, but to a complicated international apparatus of finance, trade relations, and political ties approaching a system of international barter. Let the World Bank withdraw its loans, the foreign aid programs their technical support, the industrial countries cease their trade and political rivalries, and a substantial number of countries would be helpless and hopeless as participating members of the modern community of nations.

Do the "strong" governments, mostly Communist, do better? The answer, as one might expect, is yes and no. To Western eyes the Communist states are full of contradictions. They profess the highest ethical and humanitarian intentions and use some very grim tactics in their pursuit. They use our own cherished political vocabulary—democracy, rights, equality—but give the terms meanings which bewilder us. Certainly the Communist states are not weak, measured by their tight control of police power, and their capacity to inspire in their people fanatical loyalty as well as terror is another of their contradictions.

The Communists have met with substantial success in dealing with and even advancing the capacities and complexities of modern technology. In certain areas—notably their military and space programs—their achievements have called forth wonder and anxiety. In the light of the Marxian doctrine that society should assume total responsibility for the security of the individual, what has been the record?

Here again the answer is not simple. Any judgment about the Communist system is subject to challenge, if for no other reason than because of our meager information. I shall risk one generalization: those programs oriented toward the strength of the state—nuclear power, space exploration, military strength—have been successful, while those which look primarily toward the welfare and security of the individual have lagged. The easy explanation which Communist regimes themselves make is that it has been necessary to build power rather than comfort—guns not butter, is the common cliché—but this explanation is hardly adequate. The Communist governments have included in their plans goals for housing, agriculture, transportation, and consumers' goods, as well as military goods, and these have uniformly fallen short.

I think it is fair to say that the Communists have been able to create state power as represented by military and police establishments, but they have not been equally successful in creating individual welfare or political freedom. The creation of military strength can, indeed must, be centrally directed; it must meet only one test—comparison with the corresponding strength of a potential enemy. But the creation of welfare or individual security is quite another matter. This involves the enlistment of individuals who have their own ideas of the satisfactions they want both from the work they do and the products they would prefer to enjoy. Where, as in Communist countries, these choices are made for the individual, it follows that the choices are tremendously restricted, with the inevitable consequence that interest in the result declines. In capitalist countries this range of individual choices is far wider and is left to the individual and to the employer more than to government.

The failure of the Communist system to provide the food, housing, and consumers' goods in the abundance promised squarely supports the principle that the desire of the individual to work to increase production declines as the increase becomes less and less his own. Exhortations and even threats cannot overcome the fact that human beings will work harder, save more, and risk more if the results of these efforts have some direct bearing upon a personal benefit. The tests of military strength, in which the Communists have apparently met with some success, at least are clear and definable, but the tests of a satisfactory system of individual security, in which they have been much less successful, are the diversities of human desires and preferences.

Part of the Communist failure may also be inherent in the nature of security itself as a personal and social goal. It is quite possible to exaggerate the human desire for security. Desirable as a substantial degree of security may be, a condition of total security, if such were possible, would be suffocating and intolerable. Human capacities and needs are too varied to be met by any single goal. Human beings want nothing—security, freedom, love, discipline—to the exclusion of everything else. Socially there is no pearl of great price for which everything is to be sacrificed.

Communism, by assuming control of everything for purposes of state as well as personal security, has failed to inspire the very energy such a goal requires. That some freedom is necessary to achieve security itself is being recognized now in Communist practices, even if still denied in doctrine, by the growing facts of profits, bonuses, less central direction, and more consumer freedom of choice. In Communist countries there is officially a genuine fear of freedom, but its utility is being grudgingly admitted. Perhaps the more universal lesson to be learned from Communist experience is that the dull uniformities of security are too uninspired to satisfy all human aspirations.

Between these extremes of weak and totalitarian governments lie a group whose relationships to the management of modern life are marked by neither doctrinaire socialism nor unadulterated individualism. Among these in-between countries—some nearer to and some farther from the extremes of the spectrum—are most of the countries of Western Europe and the United States.

If we take the United States as our illustration, its relationship to the problems of social security seems, at first glance, to satisfy no one. Some proponents of free enterprise see the development of social security as a threat to the growing wealth, power, and freedom in the United States. However great these achievements are, they would, these proponents believe, have been even greater if government restrictions, high taxes, and socialist programs had not imposed upon the productive machine a load greater than it is designed to carry. To them, only a dismal system of state socialism lies ahead.

On the other hand, the advocates of larger programs of social security look with discontent upon the inequalities within the American society, inequalities which they firmly equate with inequities, and see the distribution of the mounting wealth of the country as confirming evidence of injustice and human indifference. The resulting political debates have been noisy and our course of action hesitant and uncertain. There is good reason for our uncertainty. In the United States we have no such political theology to guide us as have the Communists, and we are torn between our devotion to our traditional freedom with all its utility and excitement and our humanitarian convictions that the poor and unfortunate are entitled to decent care. This conflict has been resolved, not on grounds of doctrine, but by the pragmatism of common sense.

Without aspiring to an extensive analysis of its enormous intricacy, the basic elements of the American security system might be summarized as follows: First, it is our conviction that people should be left with the greatest freedom possible as a primary condition of social, economic, and political life. Secondly, the conditions, dislocations, and adjustments of modern life require more adjustment and coordination among the factors which affect individuals than they can possibly achieve for themselves. Thirdly, government must inevitably play a substantial role in equating the burdens and benefits of a dynamic society. Thus the American social security system has emerged less as the product of social and political philosophy than as an exercise in economic calculus. We ask ourselves the question: how can the natural costs of freedom—risks and rewards of investment, invention, and obsolescence, dislocations in employment—be so absorbed as to stimulate rather than depress the gross national product, out of which all wages, profits, and benefits must be paid? In our calculations of this infinitely complex problem we have assigned an indispensable part to government.

As a part of our social and political evolution we are gradually developing a fuller understanding of some of the more subtle factors which affect the production and distribution of wealth.

Instead of a relatively simple equation of raw materials, energy, labor, and management, we are coming to see that there are other indispensable but more obscure elements. Education is a good example. We have begun to see that ignorance is simply bad business in terms of employability, lost production, and increased dependency, and that the lack of education costs more than does education itself. Where once money spent on education was looked upon as an expense, to be kept as low as possible, now we are beginning to see it as an investment, contributing to the general level of well-being. We are beginning to examine other social disabilities similarly. How much, for example, does preventable illness cost, and our answer more and more is that the illness costs more than does its prevention and cure. Illness we recognize is costly and unproductive; the care of the aged, the indigent, and the injured is a net expense to be met generously but as efficiently as possible; unemployment is a crippling interruption of income which affects not only those immediately concerned, but the good health of an entire economy. These are the understandings which lie back of legislation providing for workmen's compensation, unemployment insurance, old age assistance, "social security," and now, Medicare. Our adoption of these measures is a mixture of humanitarianism and a belief that they are also good business.

It is this quality of calculated economics more than doctrinaire philosophy which has characterized our social security legislation. This is why major extensions of security measures, in the opinion of many intelligent people, have been conservative and distressingly slow. Three elements in the equation are easily identified. The first is that people should be left as free as possible to provide for themselves rather than to have a system which would take from them both personal choice and responsibility. The second element is the belief that any plan of social security should provide only a minimum base—never as much as the individual would, through his own efforts, be expected to provide for himself. Such a base is not easy to fix; there are wide individual variations. Almost any base is sufficient to destroy for some people their slight impulse toward work. As one commentator put it: "Some people get rich awful fast." To other people the same base is only an encouraging starting point to pursue their aspirations even more aggressively. The principle of the minimum is, however, absolutely fundamental. No social security system can possibly work which makes it more profitable to be idle than to work, to be sick rather than well, to retire in order to live better.

A third concern of American legislation has been to see that the system of free enterprise was not saddled with costs it could not carry. No plan of social security is a substitute for employment; where nothing is produced, there is nothing to distribute. There has been substantial understanding, at least on the part of Congress, that it is as disastrous to destroy the incentives of business enterprise as it is to destroy the incentives of employees; but no incentives can survive unless the opportunities for their realization are genuine.

Perhaps many businessmen, conscious of heavy taxes, endless government regulations, and investment risks, will be incredulous at hearing that a genuine concern for free enterprise has actually delayed and shaped our major social security measures. Against the background of their anxieties it is understandable that each time a new proposal for an expanded program is offered there is an outcry that we are trying to provide more social security than we can afford.

At the risk of stirring fires of controversy not yet cooled, let me refer to the recent Medicare legislation. Radical as it may appear to some sections of the medical profession and of the business community, it nevertheless illustrates all of the concerns which have affected the construction of all of our security legislation. In setting a minimum it provides benefits, but the level of these benefits leaves ample room for incentives toward improvement. It provides these benefits only for those beyond sixty-five, and rejects the philosophy of the British system that a provision for illness of every kind and for all ages is the responsibility of the state at no cost to the individual. Under the American plan the average individual must contribute over many years before he is able to benefit from it at all. It is quite possible that it will stimulate the free enterprise system itself as younger people, relieved of part of the medical expense of an older generation, may spend more on their own and their children's health. At any rate, even in this latest and most furiously debated legislation there is evidence of caution—of genuine concern that we not undertake more social security than we can afford.

How much social security *can* we afford? It is not one question; it is a thousand. Experts, equally competent and intelligent, disagree, and it is a field much but not all of which should be left to experts. The reason why the average citizen has a right to share in the discussion is because all of the questions are by no means financial. They are also philosophical and political, and his views as to the kind of society he wants are important.

The real difficulty in determining how much social security a society can afford compatibly with its other values is that we can never be sure until after the fact. It is like estimating the weight which might give a machine better traction, only to find that it may actually be too heavy for the machine to carry.

The evidence in the United States is by no means conclusive, but I shall express my own opinion that, as yet, we have not undertaken more than we can afford. I am aware of the views, convincingly presented, that the true costs of social security are deferred costs and that the bill will be presented to our grandchildren later, that the plan is not an insurance plan at all but only a disguised method for the redistribution of wealth. On the other hand, these views are countered by opposing arguments equally persuasive. It is true security costs have risen rapidly, but so has the national income. To the view that the programs have been a depressant there is counter argument that social security has actually proved a stimulant to the free-enterprise system.

If social security has been merged successfully into the American economy, a very large part of the credit belongs to the American businessman. He has faced his new problems with energy and intelligence, and his willingness to run risks and assume new burdens in a revolutionary era do him much credit. A single example is sufficient. The day after the recent Medicare legislation was signed a major corporation announced its intention to build four hundred new "care centers," upon the assumption that a new base of operations had been established and that people would now want and could afford more than the new legislation provides. To me the incident speaks volumes about the nature of our society. It is an eloquent example of the relation between public action and private initiative where each leaves room for the other.

Yet social security programs are too important and too far-reaching to be careless about their extension or to view their operations with complacency. Even if we might now take the view that in the United States we have not undertaken more than we can afford, it does not mean that there is no danger that we could do so or that we may. The burdens on production can exceed capacity, and preoccupation with security can endanger necessary freedom. The equation is a delicate one. In our eagerness to abolish poverty, to lengthen life and increase comfort, it is altogether possible to undertake too much too soon.

The danger signals are visible—or at least the sources of danger. For example, have we already set some benefits so high that we have already robbed the easily content of incentives? If so, we not only add to the costs of social security, we also reduce the ability to meet them. There are also haunting questions as to the effects on business initiative. Recent reductions in taxation might well be studied not only for their stimulating effects on the economy but as to whether the previous level of taxation had not already proved a depressing overload. An illustration from the French economy may be illuminating. A French businessman facing the question of whether to add another employee must be prepared to pay not only the wages of the new employee, but also additional health, security, unemployment, and even severance pay of some 37 per cent as against some 7 or 8 per cent in the United States. Under such circumstances expansion is a serious decision. The implications for incentives and for growth seem clear for both employers and employees.

Probably the most serious and difficult problems in reconciling an effective social security system with other social factors and values are not economic but political. They test the fundamental virtues of a democracy. Where burdens are carried by one group for benefits to be given to another, conflicts of interest are inevitable. Under such circumstances doctrines of group organization and class warfare take root easily. We have our share—labor against management, country against city, consumers against producers, and now there is strain between the young and the old. While social security may be ultimately a concern common to everyone, there can be deep differences at any given time as to who pays the costs and how the benefits are to be distributed.

How, in a democratic society, can decisions affecting such a large proportion of the population so personally be made with the wisdom their importance and complexity require? Two major efforts or proposals to ensure political restraint have been made. The first consists of governmental or constitutional restraints with which Americans are generally familiar. Such restraints are based on a distribution of power—our familiar checks-and-balance system involving the states and the federal government, and the division between the executive, legislative, and judicial branches.

The second governmental device is to place the administration of complex and technical matters in the hands of experts, and beyond the immediate heat and pressure of democratic politics. Such, for example, are the Interstate Commerce Commission and the Federal Reserve Board. Neither of these devices, however, has worked in the matter of security legislation. The administration of security programs has blurred the distinctions between the states and the federal government where their independence has not disappeared altogether. Nor has Congress ever been willing to relinquish to any expert administrative agency a substantial degree of autonomy over basic decisions affecting social security.

Nor have these devices been any more effective abroad, in England, France, or the Scandinavian countries. Social security, in a democracy, has almost universal and irresistible political appeal. Any proposal promises immediate and personal benefits to many and future benefits to all; it appeals to kindly and generous impulses, and the immediate impact of costs is no more harsh than the usual "low down-payment." Such a package is almost irresistible to voter and politician alike, and the temptation is for all parties to vie with one another in putting together the largest and gayest package.

The problem of preventing excess and abuse under such circumstances is indeed difficult. Ultimately it comes to rest upon what must be the strength of any democratic society, namely, the level of its good sense and the quality of its citizenship. An incident from the early days of the New Deal will illustrate the point. The air was full of brash, impulsive, and even vindictive proposals for curing the nation's ills. Some of these involved taxation at confiscatory rates. Congressman Doughton, an old and wise man from North Carolina, was chairman of the House Ways and Means Committee, which screened all proposals. So strong was his opposition to some of those which even the administration was supporting that he went to the White House and told President Roosevelt: "Remember, Mr. President, you can shear a sheep every year; you can skin him only once." To those who object even to perpetual shearing, I suggest that it is better than being skinned—even once.

A certain level of understanding is indispensable to the operation of a social security system under democratic governments. That understanding must embrace at least two basic principles. The first is the economic one that a society cannot distribute as welfare what it does not produce as wealth. No amount of financial legerdemain can indefinitely conceal this basic fact. The other is the ethical principle of citizenship that no group can ultimately profit by pursuing its own interest to the exclusion of others. These principles may sound ethereal and even sentimental, but their acceptance may not be so impossible as the cynic may believe. Incessant education is essential, but back of education stands the harder school of experience. The current lesson in Great Britain is instructive. The Labour party, long the vehement advocate of the welfare state, finds itself calling for harder work, frugality, sacrifice in order to protect the present level of welfare. The lesson is clear that to have security there must be solvency.

The quest for security will continue to be a major personal and social preoccupation, but its pursuit ought not to obscure all other values and especially those on which security itself depends. The words of Somerset Maugham as he watched the fall of France in the first year of World War II are arresting: "Those who value security above freedom will lose their freedom, and having lost their freedom they will lose their security also."

Comment by JASPER B. SHANNON

President Stoke's imaginative paper illumines the whole subject under discussion with admirable objectivity and neutrality. To summarize a paper, itself a compact and meaty résumé of an abundance of data and a welter of ideology, is hazardous. Mercifully, we are spared any compilation of statistics so plentiful in the age of the computer. Dr. Stoke finds that contemporary man's problems arise from two sources. First, there is the inherent, built-in insecurity in human nature itself. The basic and never ending problem is that man is mortal, designed to dwell but briefly in the narrow vale between the peaks of two eternities. Imperfect man seeks an unattainable perfection. His tragic sense of life, his awareness of his eventual and inevitable rendezvous with death, his gnawing sense of inadequacy, make him seek external certitude and security. This view perhaps indicates the appropriately subconscious influence of Freud with his incisive insights into the ego and id of post-Darwinian man. In the second place, our writer tells us that imperfect and insecure man has encountered a swiftly changing environment, rapidly reconstructing the physical environment which has shaped man's nature during the millennia his species has lived on earth. His inquisitive impulse, Homo sapiens' famed bump of curiosity, has created something called science with remarkable tools for measuring and quantifying the natural world. The applications of science have created a new environment of technology which, feeding upon itself, grows with fantastic speed. Within a single lifetime we have moved from the isolated farm and insulated village to outer space, from horsepower to hydrogen energy. Historically, man is a creature of the soil.

According to widely accepted doctrines, he was created from dust, to which, very reluctantly, he must return. He has been largely a creature of the ecology of his habitat, an animal as dependent upon the earth as grasses and trees. Even as they, he takes on the protective coloration of his immediate environment.

Uprooted from their close association with the soil, men become members of the "lonely crowd" seeking identity in a brave new world of their own creation. On another occasion in human history, people, torn from their rural roots, found, first in government, the Augustan principate, a security from the turmoils of civil war and aggressive foreign conflicts. What men could not find in the government they found in a mystical future life designed to soothe frustrated spirits. When government became eventually inadequate because the will to act and to do was corroded by the acid of Socratic logic, they again returned to the soil and attached themselves to the good earth in the culturally bleak age of feudalism.

A renewed spirit of inquiry led to the discovery of America, making available millions of acres of new land which a benevolent government distributed with great abandon to all comers. Naively Thomas Jefferson believed that 160 acres of land would give such economic security to citizens as to assure them civic independence great enough to make the republic endure. Natural resources were turned over to the tender care of individual self-interest. Combined with this faith in the adequacy of man and the soil was an equally naive belief in the benevolence of the application of science to nature with a resulting unending progress. Progress with a capital *P* consisted largely in technology, or the substitution of inanimate energy for human labor in the process of economic production. Eventually, during the administration of Abraham Lincoln, a national policy was inaugurated which fostered education in agriculture and mechanics. The Morrill Act and the Emancipation Proclamation were contemporaries. One proclaimed a revolutionary doctrine that agrarian managers could not own and use their fellow men as merely private tools of production. The other expressed the simplistic hope that the application of science to the economy was an unadulterated good. An engineering term, based upon the concept of economy of energy—efficiency—was launched as a competitor for Lincoln's ethical doctrine of the government of, for, and by the people.

For a century now, the ideology of equality in politics—one man, one vote—has competed with the practice of inequality in the economy—each man for himself and the devil, or poverty, take the hindmost. As long as self-sufficing farmers had an abundance of land the two ideas had a chance to continue in two different and separate spheres somewhat as the church and the state moved in separate orbits during the Middle Ages. When the magnet had proved so attractive that free land disappeared in three generations, technology in the form of railroads induced the farmers to enter an exchange market. The forces of technology and the free market, frequently only a euphemism for competition of farmer with farmer and laborer with laborer, permitted the consolidation of the forces of credit and technology under a legal rubric called a corporation. Notwithstanding a unique effort in the United States to enforce competition by political control under the Interstate Commerce and Sherman Antitrust acts, the government lost the contest and the economy took over the driver's seat. It was not government but the economy which faltered a generation ago. Government was called upon to redress the balance between a market half free and half privately controlled. Out of this intervention the social-service state has emerged. Since the managers of corporations failed to provide security for anyone save their own management, the power of the political ballot was employed to compel economic bodies to furnish security against old age, unemployment, and now disease. Part of the cost is paid by management, part by corporate stockholders, and part by increased prices to consumers. The arrangement is somewhat rigidly operated by a cumbersome federal state trying none too successfully to cope with a centralized economy composed of feudal corporate legal entities. A New Feudalism has arisen, as

Roscoe Pound, one of Nebraska's most intelligent sons, suggested thirty-five years ago:

> In our economic order business and industry are the significant activities. They stand toward the social order of today where land-holding stood toward the social order of the Middle Ages. Every one in business, great or small, is in a shareholder relation in which things are due him as shareholder, not because of any special undertaking. He is not freely competing. The great bulk of the urban community are upon salaries and owe service to corporations which of late have sometimes shown consciousness of owing a reciprocal protection. The individual businesses are more and more giving up and going into corporate form. The corporations are more and more merging. Chain stores are bringing about a feudal organization of businesses which until now had been able to exist on the older basis. If a new domain of business or industry is opened, those who have conquered it distribute stock as a great feudal lord distributed estates. It is coming to be the general course that men do not own businesses or enterprises or industries. They hold shares in them. Moreover, as one who held several tracts of land might owe services to more than one lord, so one who holds investments may be a shareholder, with the reciprocal duties that relation implies, in more than one corporation.[1]

When corporate trustees betrayed their trust, when economic statesmanship failed, political statesmanship was called into the breach. Now we have neither a free-enterprise nor a socialistic state or economy. We have a mixed economy composed of pseudo-competitive giants operating under a credit system manipulated by an elite of businessmen and politicians with a flexibility often more pragmatic than principled. What Pound foresaw in 1930 has gained enormous momentum.

Today the typical man (for the city dweller, not the farmer is the type for this time) finds his greatness not in himself and in what he does, but in the corporation he serves. If he is great, he is published

[1] *Proceedings of the Twenty-Ninth Annual Meeting of the Kentucky Bar Association*, Louisville, Kentucky (1930), pp. 105–106.

to the world not as having this or that, but as director in this company and that.[2]

The agrarian myth of a nation of freeholders is sustained only by one outmoded farm organization. We are witnessing a new enclosure system greater than that which ended the Middle Ages. Aided and abetted by the very institutions supposedly created to advance and protect their interests, more and more farmers become rootless and landless truck drivers who find more bargaining security in the Teamsters' Union than in a farmers' organization which clings tenaciously to the ideology of the eighteenth century.

Now a nation of hired hands, we huddle together in guilds of the skilled, technologists all. All try to protect themselves from self-created competitors, computers, electronic gadgets, and mechanized monsters. The quality of our products acquires planned technological obsolescence in the process of quantity production.

As Professor Stoke suggests, we provide only a bare minimum of security. This in itself is a concession to a fear that too many hostile forces might discard the whole system and throw it to the government as has happened in so much of the world. It would be comforting to think that greater social security was productive of greater happiness; instead, the great outcries of our generation are anonymity, anxiety, alienation, annihilation, and alcoholism. The idealism of socialism has been lost in the "curse of bigness" in both industry and government. The priesthood of the psychiatrists replaces that of preachers and priests. Entrapped by both private and public collectivization based upon the Roman imperial principle of hierarchy, people find themselves doomed to frustration in a rat race of status seekers. Herbert Spencer's law of evolution from status to contract has been reversed as we move from contract to status. Rising to the top is pursued by the ruthless or inherited by the fortunate. The means of winning power by purchasing access to the media of communication, buttressed by tax-avoiding foundations, is the

[2] *Ibid.*, p. 106.

order of the day. The affluent society is accompanied by a rising tide of crime, suicides, and accidents, aside from the immediate threat of annihilation.

President Stoke enters a forceful plea for "education." He does not explicitly state whether it is to be a know-how or know-why education. He does not declare whether freedom from ignorance produces wisdom or only cunning. It is not clear whether we are to have more of the higher education which produces the values so clearly evident on Saturday afternoons in autumn, or whether it will be a self-examining education which will produce the self-mastery Jefferson pleaded for over 160 years ago. What ethos will govern the welfare state in its quest for security remains open. We know only that, as Mr. Justice Holmes so poignantly asserted two generations ago, "Certainty is an illusion and repose is not the destiny of man."

Comment by W. ROBERT PARKS

Mr. Stoke, in his discussion of "Government and the Quest for Security," has quite rightly been largely concerned with analyzing the two aspects of the relationship of government to security which, I think, are central to an understanding of the role which government can and should play in promoting individual security.

First, he has explained why modern government in an industrialized, urbanized, interdependent society must have a role in assisting the individual to find security. In his explanation of the ecology of government in the area of social security, it is made clear that it is not original sin or a selfish drive for power by an individual, group of individuals, or level of government which has pushed government into promoting the security of the individual. Rather, it has been the coercions, the new insecurities, present in our modern environment which have made it necessary for men to act through their government to protect themselves against the insecurities created by their society.

I would also like to emphasize, however, that perhaps of importance equal to the negative coercions of our environment (that is, the new insecurities) are a whole series of positive coercions set up by our new scientific knowledge and technological know-how. For these coercions of knowledge and know-how are probably as powerful in pushing government into the function of providing security as are the mere negative insecurities. It is significant, I think, that many of the insecurities which we are asking government to help protect us against today are not, in fact, new under the sun. Such insecurities as hunger, disease, and human exploitation are as old as man. What is different is that for the first time men have created a society which has the capacity to do something about them. First, we have a society which knows how to produce the abundance which leaves that margin of surplus which can be devoted to increasing almost all forms of individual security. Secondly, as a society we now have the scientific and technological knowledge with which to combat insecurities. Probably a social need is not fully created until men have the capacity to satisfy that need.

One of the clearest examples of this is, of course, in the area of health. Disease and the breakdown in the normal functioning of the human body have always been with men. Yet it is only in recent years that there has been a need for health and hospital insurance—whether it be public or private. Not until the scientific revolution in medicine had created modern medical and surgical knowledge, not until we had the scientific and technological know-how to build the modern hospital facility, was there a need to find the means by which the average man could share in these new boons to mankind.

I dwell on these new positive coercions as coequal with the new insecurities in the ecology of government and social security because I think that they should be important in shaping our attitudes on the development and use of the social mechanisms which can help to alleviate insecurity. That is, we should think of the problem of security not only from the negative view of men's having to devise the means for meeting new insecurities, but also from the positive view that, at last, society is in the fortunate position of having the knowledge and capacity to begin to solve the problem of human insecurity. Viewed in this light, the quest for security can be looked upon as a creative opportunity for human betterment, rather than simply as a reaction to a new coercion.

The second aspect of the role of government in the quest for security with which Mr. Stoke was chiefly concerned was the problem of "how much security?" How much security should government attempt to provide for the individual? How much security assistance is optimum from the standpoint of the personality and welfare of the individual recipient? How much security is optimum from the standpoint of the continuance and growth of the productive capacity of the economy? Mr. Stoke, early in his analysis, states: "We have grafted upon our inheritance from the industrial revolution the immensely greater power of modern science . . . with consequences which our slower processes of social invention find almost unmanageable."

And herein, I think, lies the central problem in the development of government's role in security. We all recognize the dangerously widening gap between scientific and technological knowledge on the one hand and social intelligence on the other. Generally, however, we relate this central problem of our times too narrowly to the issue of war and peace and the relationships between nations. Social security, however, is a good case example of the need in all areas for the use of the scientific method in building the accurate body of knowledge and facts which will permit the democratic process to choose the processes and machinery for accomplishing a given public goal.

Pluralistically, pragmatically, in a process which encompasses the rich diversities of American experience and opinion, our society has made the decision that it has some measure of responsibility for the security of the individual. Yet it still faces the immensely difficult and complex problems of determining how much security. What forms should security take, through what procedures should individual security be effectuated? Such decisions as these, affecting as they will the very structure and functioning of our whole national economy, indeed our whole society, must finally be made by the democratic process. But equally important to the welfare of all of us, these decisions must increasingly also be based upon reliable and accurate economic and social information and projections, arrived at through the scientific method. Fortunately for the future growth and development of a sound and effective system of social security, today the social sciences are taking over and adapting to their use such new tools and processes of science as applied mathematics, probability theory, and computer practice. They can, I think, increasingly be depended upon to develop the accurate body of economic and social knowledge so needed in making wise public decisions in the area of social security.

An Insurer's View

Henry S. Beers

Now chairman of the board, North American Reinsurance Companies, HENRY S. BEERS was formerly president and chairman of the board of Ætna Life Affiliated Companies and chairman of Excelsior Life, Toronto, Canada. Mr. Beers is a Fellow of the Society of Actuaries.

CURTIS M. ELLIOTT is Bert Rodgers Professor of Economics and Insurance at the University of Nebraska. A Fellow of the Society of Actuaries, JOHN C. ANGLE is vice president and actuary, Woodmen Accident and Life Company.

I feel humble in the midst of the distinguished group of men who have assembled to discuss from their respective learned and practical points of view the very vital and fundamental subject of man's quest for security. At the same time, being very proud of having spent my working lifetime in the insurance business, proud of the progress and accomplishments of the insurance business both before and during the forty-seven years that have elapsed since I entered it, I am happy indeed to try as best I can to represent insurance in these discussions.

Before going any further I have a confession to make. It was neither foresight nor logic which led to my entering the insurance business, but plain garden-variety good luck. I had fully intended, when entering college, to follow in my father's footsteps, as my younger brother later did, to become a lawyer. However, under the influence of the enthusiastic and engaging personality of my freshman math professor, I found that I loved elementary mathematics, and I proceeded to major in that subject. Then, one fateful day, this math professor told me about the mathematics examinations given by the Actuarial Society of America, how hard they were, even to the point of unfairness; that he had once tried them himself and failed, etc., etc. By the time that conversation was ended he had practically dared me to take the first two actuarial examinations, and that did it. Naturally, I took his dare and in due time, much to my surprise, I received word that I had passed; and a little later, when I wanted to start earning my own living at a time when jobs were pretty scarce immediately after World War I, I learned that life insurance companies had some jobs open for prospective actuaries, particularly if they had already passed an actuarial examination or two. So I entered the insurance business, with little knowledge of what it was like and with even less suspicion of the tremendous developments that lay ahead or of the very deep gratification that might be derived from devoting one's working lifetime to the business of man's quest for economic security.

You can understand, therefore, how I can consider myself one of the luckiest men in the world. To me, that is emphasized again today, when I find my early lack of foresight bringing me another gratifying reward—the very great pleasure of talking here about the insurance business and its part in man's quest for security.

Any great degree of economic security, or any great development of the insurance business, is well-nigh impossible except at times and in places characterized by a considerable economic and industrial development, a general respect for law and order, a basically sound currency, and reasonable stability of government. Favorable concurrences of these conditions have obviously not existed for too long; and the Roman historian Livy may not have been thinking of insurance when he wrote, some two thousand years ago, words that have been translated to say "nothing stings more deeply than the loss of money . . . and security."

On the other hand, maybe Livy did have insurance in mind when he expressed in those words man's emotional need for economic security, for he may have known that almost two thousand years before his time the Code of Hammurabi had indicated that the essentials of marine insurance were known to Babylonian traders. Hammurabi had also provided that, if a man were robbed and the criminal not apprehended, the district government would "render back to him whatsoever of his that was lost," a sort of Social Security Act. Also Livy may have known that some nine hundred years before his time, the merchants of the island of Rhodes had added important refinements to marine insurance when they devised the Rhodian Sea Law. Storms and pirates were taking their toll of trading vessels, not to mention losses due to ship-gulping sea monsters or to sailing off the edge of the world into the surrounding void. The

Rhodians designed a system whereby, when a ship failed to return, each merchant absorbed a small pro rata portion of the loss rather than allowing the unlucky individual shipowner to be ruined. We owe a great debt to the merchant chiefs of the Mediterranean, for they formalized the voluntary mutual-assistance and risk-sharing principles on which insurance is based.

The Greeks, whose reverence for human life exceeded that of any peoples who preceded them, appear to have been the first to apply these principles to men's lives. Their burial societies not only met the burial expenses of deceased members, but also provided for at least some of the temporary needs of their widows and orphans. The businesslike Romans left evidences that they had developed rather complex forms of commercial insurance and also gave continuity to the concept of life insurance through their payments to the survivors of soldiers.

Although the Greeks and Romans did make great strides forward in the discovery of insurance principles and in the wider application of these principles, to more people, they brought increased security to no more than rather small fractions of the population. In times of adversity, the great majority still had to rely for their economic necessities on the by no means certain good will and generosity of their relatives and neighbors, who themselves might or might not have any resources to share.

The snail's-pace development of man's cooperative efforts at achieving economic security halted altogether with the fall of Rome to the barbarians and the advent of the Dark Ages. Feudalism is sometimes characterized as a compulsory form of security: in return for his loyalty and labor a man hoped to obtain protection and the necessaries of life for himself and his family. This was not an ennobling form of security—and it existed only at the whim of the lord of the manor and only so long as the latter remained as strong as or stronger than his rivals. This insecure form of security, so shocking to us today, may still compare favorably with the situation of a significant proportion of contemporary mankind, living in countries not yet characterized by any considerable economic and industrial development, respect for law and order, soundness of currency, or stability of government.

The Renaissance marked the rebirth of mutual-assistance efforts on the part of Western man. The merchant and artisan guilds, later the Friendly Societies of England, other groups in other places, all used insurance concepts to protect the security of their members.

The Great Fire of London in 1666, while enormously destructive, had two beneficial side effects: one, it destroyed that section where the plague that periodically swept the city was concentrated, and this has been credited with curtailing the future outbreaks of the disease; two, fire insurance sprang into being from its embers, enabling men to protect their homes from the financial consequences of the disaster of fire.

Then life insurance policies and annuities entered the scene—often, in the early days, woefully underpriced or overpriced by reason of misconceptions as to the principles involved. Efforts to clear up these misconceptions led to the emergence of actuarial science, dealing with the mathematics of life contingencies, that is, the probabilities of life and death, which were for long greatly misunderstood. They are still surprisingly mysterious to many, despite the fact that all of the really basic principles of actuarial science had been developed and logically presented in textbooks by the time I became an actuarial student forty-odd years ago.

This reference to my early actuarial-student days reminds me of what probably ought to have been the frightening story I read at the time about an actuary who was such a complete actuary that he filled many notebooks with statistical observations of all sorts of phenomena concomitant with life and death, attempting to analyze these phenomena mathematically and thus extend the frontiers of his actuarial understanding and knowledge. In today's terminology we'd very likely say that this had a psychosomatic effect, for at a ripe but not terribly advanced age he discovered one day while analyzing his notebooks that he had for some time been sleeping longer each night than the night before, fifteen minutes longer to be precise. This continued. The time arrived when he slept for twenty-three hours and forty-five minutes. On awakening, he hastily called his wife, children, and grandchildren about him, gave them such advice as the wisdom of a lifetime suggested, and bade them an affectionate farewell. At the end of fifteen waking minutes, he promptly fell asleep again, slept for precisely twenty-four hours, and quietly expired. To my youthful mind that was a highly admirable example of complete absorption in one's chosen profession. Now that I am older, I confess that I feel happy to observe that my sleep habits show no disquieting regularity.

Actuarial science, as I have indicated, was a very mature science when I came to it, and I promptly became convinced that all of the life insurance problems of the future could be solved by the experience and wisdom of the past. These *have* supplied the basic and immutable principles, but the actual developments and innovations in my lifetime were to be so extraordinary that no one would then have conceived them to be possible of accomplishment in a short half-century.

One might have expected a gradual improvement in death rates, but the unprecedentedly rapid drops in mortality rate and the blessed conquests of many killing diseases have been beyond anything that could have been credible in forecast.

No one fifty years ago would have guessed to what extent new policies could be developed to provide new packages of life insurance and annuity benefits, "new" even if the elements of each package were as old as actuarial science; and no one would have foreseen the development of new uses for life insurance in the business world, such as to protect businesses in the event of death of key executives, or to provide necessary additional security for loans, or to assure orderly continuance of partnership businesses after the death of one partner, and so on and so forth.

Group life insurance was in its early infancy fifty years ago. A wise man would have been optimistic of its survival in the insurance world; but who would have been so rash as to predict that it would become a major economic and social force covering, as it does today, four out of every five employees in the

United States, in groups both large and small? The volume of group life insurance now in force is twelve times the total volume of all kinds of life insurance fifty years ago (and the volume of individual life insurance in force is still double that of group).

During the past fifty years there have been extraordinary changes in the methods by which life insurance is presented to the purchaser, now enabling him to analyze his financial situation and buy the particular policies that fit into a logical program of protection for the particular insurance needs of his own family. This outstandingly valuable programming approach, together with other improved procedures and strengthened standards of competence, have happily changed the public image of life insurance agents from that of rather ineffectual but annoyingly high-pressure salesmen, often failures in other lines of endeavor (all too generally a true picture fifty years ago), to now, in many cases, trusted confidential advisers of quasi-professional or professional stature.

Insurance is said to add a "time utility," as it were, to a person's money. Premiums are paid with "normal" dollars, when the insured has an income to pay them from; benefit dollars are received when adversity makes the need for dollars acute, perhaps desperately acute, which makes their value much greater, sometimes beyond measure.

The peril insured against may be death, for which there is life insurance; or it may be long life, for which there are annuities to pay retirement incomes after one's working years; or it may be sickness, for which we have health insurance. These are only three in a long list of insurable perils; but I would like to defer mention of the rest in order to talk for a while about the growth I have, in my own working lifetime, been privileged to observe in the health insurance field.

I can even now well remember commencing to study the subject of health insurance in preparation for the actuarial examination on that subject. The literature was discouraging—it could hardly have been more so if every page had been headed in red ink "Danger—keep out!" A small amount of health insurance was then in force, mostly under policies paying weekly or monthly incomes during disability, but even that had been enough to provide some striking examples of the subjective nature of many disabilities and of malingering among the heavily insured. One actuary wrote savagely that to collect on fire insurance it was necessary to prove a fire, and to collect on life insurance it was necessary to prove a death, but that to collect on health insurance it was necessary only to have a policy! Although there then seemed to be ample evidence to justify this negative attitude, that didn't stop insurance companies from continuing to try one health insurance experiment after another, until today four out of every five Americans carry one or more forms of health insurance. This is really extraordinary in view of the unprofitable nature of many forms of health insurance even up to the present time. The explanation is that there is a very strong public demand for the security that health insurance gives and competition has responded with offers of coverage. To look at another and very important aspect of the matter, claim payments under hospital, surgical, medical, and other health insurance policies have been of vital help in paying for and thus helping make possible in this country the highest standards of medical care in the world.

It is easy to say that an ordinary or routine responsibility of every business is to adapt itself to meet new situations in our ever changing world, but I submit that an outstandingly admirable example of that stands to the credit of health insurance. And now, of course, further innovation and change is required to adapt to another markedly new situation. Whether wisely or not—and it will be a long time before agreement is reached on that question—Congress has enacted a Medicare bill to provide health-care benefits to millions of social security beneficiaries and other aged people.

While Medicare's long-term effect on the insurance business remains to be seen, I am confident that insurers will adjust themselves to this "new situation in our ever changing world." The graver danger that this legislation may be an omen of the ultimate nationalization of all health insurance is, I believe, a remote one that the American public would not approve nor

Congress enact. My feelings are naturally hurt that the perfectly amazing and unprecedented accomplishment of the insurance business during recent decades in extending health insurance to a rapidly increasing proportion of the aged has gone unrecognized except for the preposterous label of "too little and too late." In actuality, progress had been too fast to be anything approaching always wise or profitable, and a continuance of this experimentation (this very productive, albeit slightly reckless, experimentation) was clearly in the public interest. Well, as I said, my feelings are hurt, but I will find my own crying towel and add my voice to those who say, "Here is a new situation in our ever changing world. Let's concentrate our efforts on anticipating new trends and on developing the kinds of insurance the new world needs and will buy. That must ever be our contribution to man's quest for security."

The insurance business is usually counted among the very "conservative" institutions in our economic and social life. It must be conservative, because it is a "trust" sort of operation in which, above all else, policyholders' reserves must be safeguarded and adequate funds maintained to assure claim payments to all those who are going to suffer the losses insured against. While the insurance man's need to be conservative may somewhat too often condition him to oppose desirable, even inevitable change, it is extremely difficult in the modern business world for any insurance or other business organization to maintain the status quo. In fact, an obsession with security through the maintenance of the status quo is the enemy of long-term profit and even existence. It must be replaced by an intense desire to respond to the new situations arising in our ever changing world. Insurance history provides many happy examples of such response.

Marine insurance, generally thought to be the oldest insurance line, may still use much archaic language in its policy (for example, still giving protection against "... perils ... of the seas, men-of-war, fires, enemies, pirates, rovers, thieves, jettisons, letters of mart and countermart, reprisals, takings at sea, arrests, restraints and detainments of all kings, princes, or people, of what nation, condition or quality soever, barratry of the master and mariners . . ."), but actual marine insurance practices of today are the result of numberless changes in transportation that have taken place during the centuries since some of the present policy wording was first drafted.

The several kinds of insurance which present-day trade, business, and industry need, or which the present-day homeowner needs, used to be divided into much neater and simpler compartments than would be convenient today, with sharp distinctions between life, health, accident, fire, burglary, plate glass, several separate kinds of liability insurance, several separate kinds of automobile insurance, ocean marine, inland marine, etc., etc. Modern requirements are for broader packages and a correspondingly "packaged" organization of underwriting and production-supervision, which are being arrived at through a difficult and often painful process of competitive experimentation and adjustment. Quite apart from the ordinary course of business, recent decades have brought many special situations affecting man's quest for economic security which have taxed all our insurance ingenuity, to put it mildly.

Great medical discoveries have brought to mankind the great boon of powerful but expensive means of cure. That word "expensive" has given health insurance some exceedingly difficult and painful problems to solve. However discouraging this has been, insurers have responded with new benefits and provisions to meet the changing requirements.

For a long time during the early days of life insurance in this country, policies became null and void if the insured traveled too far from home, into the then unhealthy or dangerous regions of the southern and western states, or into less settled parts of the world. In the days when horses and wagons were the usual means of land transportation, railroad engineers, firemen, and conductors had to pay extra for life insurance protection; and anybody with nerve enough to serve as brakeman on a freight train just couldn't get insurance. Similarly, it was years after Kitty Hawk before aviators and their passengers could get life insurance that covered them in flight.

In contrast, a week before Major Gordon Cooper blasted off on a twenty-two-orbit space flight in 1963, the Ætna Life Insurance Company issued a $100,000 life insurance policy to Cooper and to each of the six other original astronauts; their coverage was good anywhere on earth or in outer space.

When exploration of peaceful uses of atomic energy began, another new need was created for insurance protection. Accident and liability coverages had to be provided in enormous amounts because of the huge investments in plants and equipment, and because one accident involving radioactive material could conceivably render an entire area uninhabitable for years—to say nothing of the more than profound effect it could conceivably have on the present and future population of the area. No single insurance company was strong enough to provide sufficient coverage for even one nuclear plant. The insurance business responded by forming special underwriting associations in which the resources of many companies are pooled to provide unprecedented amounts of protection.

A less recent and less spectacular instance of pooling made it possible for the insurance business to provide the accident and liability protection needed by the airlines for their passenger and freight air transport. The seemingly prohibitive risks involved in insuring what were then "large" planes (carrying, say, fourteen or twenty-one passengers) happily led to the formation of pools, which more recently have somehow managed to develop the capacity to cover the values and liabilities of the modern jets and may, all too soon for insurance conservatism, have to find the capacity to underwrite the coming supersonic transports.

While these pools are presently under antitrust attack, for reasons that to me are not yet very clear, it is devoutly to be hoped that such changes, if any, as are legally necessary in their organization or operation will not take away the insurance world's ability to meet the insurance requirements of these future SST's.

There are a great many other details of the insurance business and of insurance history that I could be tempted to discuss with you. The time has come, however, when I must move into the final phase of my discussion of the part that insurance plays in man's quest for security—in helping him achieve economic security.

Does this economic security mean protection against change in man's economic condition, to enable him to maintain the status quo? Not by any means: we must not forget the paradox that an obsession with security through the maintenance of the status quo is the enemy not only of all progress but also ultimately of security itself.

Even if it seems to raise another paradox, let me try to explain how insurance, by protecting the status quo against certain risks, can enable a prudent man to incur other and perhaps greater risks in order to progress far beyond the status quo. A few examples may indicate what I mean.

Life insurance has provided many a man's widow and orphans with their main or only means of self-respecting subsistence. Often it alone has enabled the members of the bereaved family to remain in what may be called their own world, something near to the kind of life they have been used to, with some of the comforts and amenities of our civilization in addition to the necessaries of life, and with the right kind of opportunities for the bringing up and the education of the children. That is one side of the life insurance coin: the other is that the ownership of an adequate amount of life insurance enables a prudent man to incur larger financial obligations and to take greater financial risks for the furtherance of his career and, if he is successful, for the ultimate benefit and satisfaction of his family. He can do so in reliance on life insurance to pick up his financial responsibilities to his family if death interrupts his attainment of his business or professional objectives. The tendency of recent decades toward early marriages and having children young gains a measure of economic prudence when life insurance is present; the parents of a young girl can even prepare for this by buying insurance on her life with the provision that, if and when she marries, she can transfer it to the life of her bridegroom.

Fire insurance has in numberless instances prevented personal or business insolvency when a home or factory has burned down, and insolvencies are catastrophes not only to the owners who lose their investments but also to many others, including suppliers, employees, and whoever are wholly or largely dependent on the continuance of the business. The other side of the fire insurance coin is that neither individuals nor businesses would, without fire insurance, dare to build the homes or business and industrial plants and complexes that add so much to the comforts and efficiency of present-day life and to the productivity of the modern economy. Also, nearly all building today is done with the help of borrowing, and the requirement of fire insurance assigned to the lender is routine.

We know a great deal about the forces of nature—but we have not learned how to prevent hurricanes, or tornadoes, or earthquakes; so society needs insurance against these natural perils, as well as the perils arising out of automobiles, airplanes, and the nuclear and other new engines of transportation and production that man invents.

We are learning something, all too slowly, about the mind of man and about mental disease, but crime still takes a vast economic toll; and the lesser sin of carelessness exposes us individually or in our businesses not only to costly damages to ourselves and our properties but also to various and sometimes staggering liabilities to others.

Insurance provides a bulwark against these hazards to economic security, bulwarks it would be unthinkable to be without; for economic misfortune rarely, if ever, affects only the few persons whom it directly strikes. If there is no method of relieving the financial consequences of individual catastrophe, society as a whole suffers both from the nonpayment of the liabilities of the insolvent and from the interruption of the productive activities of all concerned. And the other side of the coin is that, in the absence of the security that insurance can promise, man would not dare to invest either his money or his efforts in the business and personal activities and operations which make the modern world what it is and lead to the great developments which the passing decades observe.

It is estimated that the industrialized countries of the world account for some 90 per cent of the world's insurance-premium income, though they comprise only 30 per cent of the world's population. At the beginning of my talk I made the point that much insurance or economic security of any kind is possible only in places characterized by a considerable economic and industrial development. Now I stress the other side of the coin, that insurance assists in this development and that without insurance the pace of our economic and industrial development would be slow indeed.

I should like to conclude with a short commentary on the insurance business's own quest for security. How can the insurance business insure itself? I do not at this point have in mind the technical, but nonetheless important, matter of protection through reinsurance against too large claims or catastrophic aggregations of claims. What I am thinking about is the long-term security of the insurance business. This must come from its adaptability to change; from the *new* protections it provides against the financial consequences of the *new* hazards and perils which our country's developing economic and personal life incurs; from the extent to which the security provided by insurance to business and industry, and individuals, makes it prudent for business and industry, and individuals, to exercise the boldness and adventurousness which a good pace of economic and personal progress will always require.

I hope for the insurance business, as I hope for all business, and in fact for man himself, no security that is not grounded on courageous and wise adaptation to the new situations that our ever changing world will present.

Comment by Curtis M. Elliott

Mr. Beers discussed the role of the insurance principle in man's quest for security. He pointed briefly to the early uses of the principle, particularly in marine ventures, and to the need for a high degree of economic and industrial development, a general respect for law and order, a basically sound currency, and reasonable stability of government before the principle could have a widespread use. Reference was made to developments in health, property, and life insurance as indications that the insurance industry's progress is paralleling that of basic economic and social change. He concludes that the long-term security of the industry, perhaps as a private institution, must come from its success in providing a greater degree of security for those risks that can be brought under the aegis of the insurance principle.

There are many facets of the use of the insurance principle that Mr. Beers did not discuss. This, we can be certain, was not due to oversight, but to time limitations.

In Western civilization to a great extent, and in the United States to a limited degree, the insurance principle has been used extensively in social insurance. Its adaptability to fundamental risks that are not subject to treatment by private insurance carriers, or to risks for which the industry has had difficulty in making provision, is an important use of the principle in man's quest for security. Mr. Beers does mention the recently legislated Medicare program with the strong implication that the health insurance industry was not at fault in failing to provide for the health insurance needs of the American people. He cites the fact that four out of every five persons have purchased one or more health insurance contracts, and this is used as evidence that the health industry has made sincere and valiant attempts to solve the problem of insecurity of the aged with respect to the costs of medical services, hospital, and other related expenses. This conclusion may be subject to some debate. That four out of five persons have some form of health insurance is an indication only of volume. It is not an indication of the extent to which the aged alone have coverage or an indication of the completeness of the coverage for the average policyholder.[1] We must recognize that there are limitations in the application of the insurance principle by the private insurance industry and, with respect to major fundamental risks, the use of the principle in social insurance constitutes a unique and perhaps a much more satisfactory method of solving the problem of insecurity than most other methods of handling the risk. Mr. Beers could have discussed the application of the principle to social insurance programs more extensively.[2]

Mr. Beers is to be congratulated for not using the favorite criticism of the uninitiated that social insurance programs are actuarially unsound. These people reason that if the program is actuarially unsound, then it must be a mistake. If the assumption is, then, that all types of private insurance are actuarially sound, the critic has much to learn about premium determination methods in automobile, fire, general liability, and many other forms of property and casualty insurance. In many cases, actuarial soundness is hardly more than enlightened judgment tempered with some rather crude statistical information. Actuarial soundness is also an important problem in individual life annuities and in disability income coverages in life insurance.

The insurance industry must, we may assume, be conservative. However, it should constantly experiment with new

[1] If, on the average, only a portion of the expenses incurred are paid under these contracts, the problem of insecurity in the health insurance risk is still a major problem.

[2] Mr. Beers accepts the Medicare program, even though he deplores its passage. Unlike many of his colleagues, however, he does not feel that the program will expand into universal coverage for the American people.

coverages and new applications of the insurance principle to risks that heretofore have been considered uninsurable. If it is to continue to play a significant role in man's quest for security, it must be progressive.

The insurance industry in the United States has had a phenomenal, almost incredible, growth. This does not mean, however, that it is not open to criticism for many shortcomings. It is subject to criticism for many practices which, if not corrected, will mean that its proper role in man's quest for security is being neglected. As an illustration of the neglect of an important risk, we had the virtual exit of the life insurance industry from income disability coverages after the fiasco in the decade of the 1920's and the early '30's. Rather than attempt to provide the insurance on a financially sound basis, the industry followed the simple expedient of ignoring the risk altogether. Somewhat the same problem existed in the underwriting of individual life annuity contracts after the significant increase in the demand for this coverage arose in the early 1930's. Because mortality changes were difficult to prognosticate and because they reacted unfavorably to the insurance carrier, the easiest course to follow was that of ignoring almost completely the development of individual life annuities.

Much of the unprogressiveness of the industry has been a result of the insistence in the United States, until recent times, of the use of the mono-line rather than the multiple-line principle of company organization. It has also been the result of the shortsighted insistence of insurance regulatory authorities upon a high degree of standardization of insurance coverage and premium rates. If the industry is to keep pace with basic economic and social changes, it must be permitted to underwrite all the insurance needs of individuals and businesses, and its efforts in the direction of experimentation with new contracts should not be thwarted by the insistence upon a high degree of standardization. Perhaps it is time to analyze our regulatory legislation critically and make the changes necessary to permit the industry to proceed in a more progressive manner. Complete multiple-line legislation, under which an insurance carrier will be allowed to underwrite all types of insurance, can be a significant and progressive step. Perhaps a modification in property and casualty insurance of the prior-approval laws, allowing the carriers more leeway in filing and using rates and in initiating new and broader contracts, would also be important. This means that more dependence will be placed upon competition as the regulatory force rather than upon relatively arbitrary control standards.

Regulation has been slow in recognizing basic developments that require significant changes in coverages and practices. But the industry has also been far too conservative in its approach to several important current risks. An excellent example is the risk of flood. Flood can involve many people and businesses in catastrophic financial losses, yet the industry has accomplished little in providing insurance coverage for this risk. Innumerable discussions and many proposals have been made in the past twenty years for a solution of this problem by the private insurance industry, but little progress has been made in making possible the insuring of the risk from a practical standpoint. The industry virtually admits that it cannot provide insurance for this risk on a widespread basis, yet it remains antagonistic to almost every effort to promulgate a governmental program of flood insurance. If the industry cannot solve a problem by its application of the insurance principle, it should admit its inadequacies and allow the insurance principle to be used in a program of social insurance.

There are many additional examples of the slowness of the industry in the development of new and modern insurance coverages. The puny efforts in the development of all-risks crop insurance can be cited as an illustration. The slowness in developing personal and commercial package insurance contracts with monthly premium payments is another. There is no reason why a business unit should not be able to obtain all its property and casualty insurance needs in one policy, from one insurance carrier, and through one insurance agent. In addition, there is no reason why the policy should not include all types of group insurance—life, disability, and hospitalization—with the exception, perhaps, of pensions. In many instances much of the property insurance in this contract would be written with sizable deductibles.[3]

In many instances an overly zealous and highly competitive industry may cause many of its own problems. Most of the problems of the homeowners policies are a consequence of a liberality which is inconsistent in an industry that must adhere to a relatively conservative approach. If extremely liberal policy forms are promulgated and marketed at inadequate premium rates and with little regard to insurance to value, difficulties must arise. Retrenchments in coverage and the demand for sizable premium increases do not contribute significantly to the public image of the industry. The same is true of automobile insurance. The inadequacies in premium rates produced by the competitive struggle of the Bureau companies to regain business that was permitted to go to independents some years ago has made a fiasco of automobile insurance. This could result in a partial socialization of this type of insurance.[4]

The insurance industry in the United States must attain a greater degree of maturity so that it can, in the words of Mr. Beers, "become adaptable to change and so that it can provide the protection for new hazards which our country's developing economic and personal life incurs." Its real contribution to man's quest for security must depend upon its ability and willingness to develop new and broader insurance coverages so that more and more of the personal and business risks will be subject to the insurance principle.

[3] The slowness of the industry to respond to change may be cogently illustrated by the fact that large deductibles in fire and allied perils insurance have become available only recently in Bureau filings.

[4] There are many persons today who feel that the chaos in automobile insurance may well be the entering wedge for federal regulation of the insurance industry.

Comment by JOHN C. ANGLE

Mr. Beers outlines the history of insurance in the Western world and discusses the contribution that insurance makes to human security and to the stability of our economy. In reviewing his life in the insurance business, he recalls the more significant changes that he has seen, most of them as unpredictable at the time he entered the business as the course of history itself. It is striking, I think, that Henry Beers chose not to recite massive statistics as to the assets of insurance companies or as to the portion of the population insured against each risk to which the human being is susceptible. Rather, he has dwelt upon innovation and change and is saying to those of us within the insurance world that the long-term health and growth of the insurance business must come about through adaptability to change. He admonishes us that "an obsession with security through the maintenance of the status quo is the enemy of long-term profit and even existence."

Henry Beers is well aware that we live in a time in which the rate of change seems to accelerate with each passing year, when new discoveries appear with bewildering speed to make obsolete those principles which were, a few years back, acknowledged as basic truths.

He became a Fellow of the Actuarial Society of America in 1923. During the following years he assumed increasingly greater responsibilities with the Ætna Companies. Twenty years after the attainment of his fellowship, Mr. Beers somehow found time to present four papers to actuarial bodies: one concerned an aspect of mortality investigations and three were mathematical in nature, offering new formulas for interpolation, a process that allows one to calculate intervening values of a mathematical function when one knows the values at widely spaced intervals. Yet with the passage of twenty years, actuarial interest in the science of interpolation has lessened considerably as computers have made it a simple matter to compute values of the most complex mathematical functions for any range of variables desired.

An organization named the Society of Actuaries is the present-day successor to the body that admitted Mr. Beers to fellowship in 1923. The organization has grown and changed considerably over the years in response to changes in actuarial science. Today over 10 per cent of 1,450 Fellows of the Society serve as members of, or advisors and consultants to, its Education and Examination Committee that holds examinations and provides instructional material for students of the Society. The transactions of this organization continue to increase in size as we find ourselves not exempt from the knowledge explosion of our times.

It is important to say that insurance does not eliminate risk. Each of us is certain to die, and no amount of life insurance will postpone by even a day the date of our death. But what about the loss of the weekly paycheck upon which wife and children depend, should we die? This risk can be eliminated by purchase of life insurance that will assume the place of the paycheck if the wage earner dies. Insurance does aid man in his quest for security by diminishing or eliminating many of the economic impacts of risk.

Insurance delivers man from the paralysis of uncertainty caused by some insurable hazard and allows him to enter upon many activities he would not contemplate in the absence of insurance. It is only with the financial consequences of collision, fire, and death eliminated that we feel free to drive an automobile, to buy a home, or to marry and raise a family. As Mr. Beers points out, it is quite prudent for a young couple to begin a family when life insurance is present to guarantee that the children can be raised and educated even though the couple has meager savings.

A discussion of the place of insurance in man's quest for security leads inevitably to the institutions that issue insurance.

Have insurers kept pace with the changes of the day? I would reply that the record of the insurance business has been a good one, although no record of past triumphs supports much complacency within the industry. Those who rest on their laurels soon find themselves left far behind.

The personal insurance industry is in fact 1,585 separate life insurance companies. No one insurer dominates the industry, and differences of opinion as to pricing and forms of coverage are evident in almost all types of insurance. Ours is a most competitive industry in which companies continually vie to provide improved service to gain the attention of the buyer. Competition is a far better spur to efficient operation than any possible regulatory legislation.

Insurers of today are well aware of the evolutionary changes affecting them and their policyholders. Medicare will bring about a significant reorientation of insurers to provide improved forms of health insurance to those under age sixty-five. One today hears more discussions of means of improving operations than ever before. As one example, the industry has been a pioneer in the use of data processing equipment.

Insurance is subject to extensive state regulation. The insurance codes of most states cover hundreds of pages and spell out in great detail what an insurer can and cannot do. The primary thrust of these laws is to make certain that an insurer is financially able to provide the benefits promised in its contracts of insurance. Unfortunately, laws sometimes tend to stifle innovation and to discourage constructive changes necessary in today's world. One hopes that regulatory officials will understand the need for sympathetic treatment of new ideas which may not always fit the mold of the business of yesteryear.

These comments would not be complete without mention of the contribution to man's quest for security made by the men who sell insurance. Insurance is widely owned only because able, dedicated people have sought out those who have needed insurance, skillfully explaining the benefits that insurance has to offer and completing the necessary contract between insured and insurer. Without such efforts, most persons would never buy needed insurance.

An Economist's View

Charls E. Walker

CHARLS E. WALKER is executive vice president of the American Bankers Association. Mr. Walker, who holds a Ph.D. in economics from the University of Pennsylvania, taught at the Wharton School in 1948 and at the University of Texas (1950–1954). From 1954 to 1961 he was associated with the Federal Reserve Bank in Dallas, serving as vice president and economic advisor, and also with the Republic National Bank in the same city, where he was economist and assistant to the president. During 1959–60 he was on leave as assistant and principal economic advisor to the Secretary of the Treasury. He has written articles for professional journals and contributed to books in the field of economics.

CAMPBELL R. MCCONNELL, who is a professor of economics at the University of Nebraska, is the author of *Economics: Principles, Problems and Policies* (1963). WALTER S. HENRION is vice president and treasurer of Woodmen Accident and Life Company.

I shall consider three questions: First, how do economic arrangements, institutions, and attitudes bear upon man's quest for security? Second, with respect to the United States, how well are these economic arrangements functioning in helping man in his search for security? Third, what are the prospects for good economic performance in the future?

THE ECONOMIC PROBLEM

To the economist, man's quest for security can be translated into his efforts to solve the economic problem that confronts any society: Man's material wants, for all practical purposes, are unlimited, but the means of satisfying those wants are relatively scarce. Such scarcity exists because in all but the crudest societies the goods that satisfy man's material wants are produced from some combination of natural resources, labor, and capital equipment—the so-called factors of production—all of which are relatively scarce. Economics is often described as the study of how man goes about using the scarce means available to best satisfy his unlimited wants. The combination of economic arrangements, rules, institutions, and techniques can be thought of as the economic organization or framework within which this effort is made.

The type of economic organization existing at any given time will necessarily be complex, but its major characteristics will be few. For example, emphasis may be placed upon producing goods in the simplest, most direct fashion, or emphasis may instead be on roundabout methods of production, taking maximum advantage of power and equipment, with workers specializing in narrow tasks—if the latter, the technique of production is said to be roundabout or indirect. The more roundabout a system of production, the more complex the other aspects of economic organization are likely to be.

Another important characteristic of economic organization pertains to the ownership of the natural resources and equipment that enter into production. If owned by the people as a whole through the state, the system is "socialistic." If owned by the people individually or in groups, it is a "private," "free-enterprise," or "capitalistic" system.

Still another fundamental characteristic of economic organization relates to the decision-making process: who determines what is to be produced, when, and in what amount? In socialism, with the factors of production owned by the government, such decisions usually are made by state officials, who may or may not attempt to meet the preferences of the general public. In a system of private ownership, such decisions usually are made by the owners of the factors of production, who in turn try to respond to the demands and desires of those who purchase their products. Such desires are transmitted to the producers through the price system. This system is one of free choice, reflecting freedom of decision on the part of both producers and consumers, and implying that, except for those areas closely controlled or influenced by government (such as national defense), the consumer directs economic resources into the lines of production he prefers.

Economic organization in any advanced society will be much more complex than here described. Still, these three characteristics go a long way toward describing any economic system. As applied to the advanced industrial nations of the Western world, it is apparent that the dominant type of economic organization is free-choice capitalism, with the factors of production owned and directed by individuals or groups of individuals, not by the state, and prices determined by competitive factors (although this varies considerably among the nations). This type of system is often referred to as a market economy, and I shall so refer to it in this paper.

It is no accident that the market economy is common to the Western democracies, for freedom of political choice and freedom of economic choice go hand in hand—neither can exist for long without the other. This does not mean that Western governments do not play a large role in the economic affairs of their societies; quite the contrary. But the fact remains that the fundamental driving force in each instance emanates not from the state but from the individuals and private organizations that participate in the market process.

Criteria for Judging Economic Performance

What do we expect from the United States economy today? How well is it meeting these expectations? Efficiency, equity, capacity for facilitating growth, and stability—these may be viewed as the four major criteria for judging the performance of an advanced market economy in the 1960's.

Efficiency. Given the nature of the economic problem—scarce resources and unlimited wants—the need for efficiency in producing and distributing goods and services goes almost without saying. It is easy to lose sight of this goal in an economy as wealthy as that of the United States. Moreover, it is easy to recite many examples of what seem to be wasteful use of resources.[1] But the fact remains that the U.S. economy is by definition the most efficient the world has ever known. The proof of the pudding is in the eating, for the final test of economic efficiency is the capacity of an economy to turn out goods and services.

[1] What appears to be wasteful in the short run may actually promote output in the long run. An unsuccessful venture into a new enterprise may appear to be wasteful, since it uses up resources without turning out goods and services, but in many instances such ventures help maintain competition in the short run as well as point the way to successful ventures in the future. In this sense, such a venture may be viewed as analogous to an unsuccessful effort in a series of laboratory experiments which finally lead to success.

Also, what is "wasteful" production to one person may be highly useful to another. In a free-choice economy, the consumer—within limits established by society—calls the tune, and the only meaningful test of usefulness is therefore in the marketplace.

Efficiency in a free-choice economy refers not only to the maintenance of low costs and high output; such an economy should also be reasonably responsive to the changing demands of consumers. Any shift in demand reflecting changes in consumer preferences should be transmitted to producers through the price and profit mechanism. Producers would then be expected to shift resources into the most profitable lines, thereby assuring that consumer preferences are met. Although this picture is highly simplified, a study of the ebb and flow of industrial eminence in the United States over the years will clearly bear out the tendency for our market economy to respond in this way.

Efficiency also requires responsiveness on the part of producers to changes in technology. Producers must be receptive to new methods and new machinery. Such receptiveness not only promotes low-cost output in the short run, but also facilitates economic growth.

A properly functioning market economy automatically promotes the types of efficiency discussed here; indeed, this is one of the most important advantages it possesses over other types of economic organization. In a market economy, it is the inefficient producer who sustains losses and the inefficient worker who earns the least. The efficient producer finds that either his costs are lower or his product is better. In either event, he is better able to compete, and his profits improve. The efficient worker finds it easier to hold a job and earn good wages. It is therefore very much in the self-interest of both the producer and the worker to be efficient. To the extent this works out in practice, the fundamental human trait of self-interest is harnessed to contribute to the general good.

But it does not always work out this way in practice, primarily because of what economists refer to as market power, or simply inadequacy of competition. Efficiency depends upon competition. This does not mean that large-scale enterprise must be disallowed; quite the contrary, the economies of large-scale production, if not permitted to tend toward monopoly, can provide rich dividends for consumers in the form of efficiency in output. It does mean that vigorous but fair administration of the antitrust laws is indispensable to the efficient operation of a market economy. Monopolistic powers of labor unions can also severely damage efficiency, as well as threaten the stabilization goals of a market economy.

Equity. Equity in the distribution of income lies pretty much in the eyes of the beholder. But, whether right or wrong, the very definition of a market economy presupposes a definition of equity in income distribution, namely, that each participant in the productive process should receive income in precise proportion to his contribution to that process.

Now, no Western democracy will completely accept this ruthless approach to income distribution. But it is essential to recognize that governmental attempts to redirect income run the serious risk of impairing the efficiency which is one of the fundamental strengths of the market economy. Certain types of income redirection (e.g., high income tax rates on the productive worker with the funds thus captured used to provide a subsidy for the less productive) may dull incentive and lead to less total output for the economy as a whole. Income redistribution such as that exemplified by our agricultural price support program may actually increase efficiency in the subsidized industry, but only at the cost of the inefficiencies of misdirected effort and resources.

Question should be raised as to what extent inequities in income distribution are attributable to the way a market economy operates as opposed to other factors. One of the most important of these other factors is discrimination, which for many of our citizens forecloses adequate opportunity for jobs or for the education and training increasingly essential in today's economy. The economist can point to the economic aspects of this problem; and, as a citizen, he can recognize it as probably the most serious domestic problem now confronting our nation. But the roots of the problem stem not from the fundamental characteristics of a market economy. In fact, equality of opportunity is one of the requisites of an efficiently functioning market economy. It follows that the solutions to the problem are not to be found in changing the basic framework of our economic organization, but in other ways. The economist recognizes, however, that failure to deal effectively with the problem could have severe economic consequences.

Capacity for Facilitating Growth. Whereas efficiency and equity have long been viewed as desirable attributes of an economic system, it is only in recent years that emphasis has been placed on growth as an important economic goal.[2] The record in the United States speaks for itself, but this does not mean that high and sometimes spectacular rates of growth cannot be achieved in nonmarket economies. This is especially true in a system in which state officials are able to direct a large portion of current production toward growth-producing investment, as has been the case in the Soviet Union.[3] There is real question, however, as to whether such forced draft efforts are sustainable over time. Indeed, in recent years there have been more and more indications from the Soviet Union of less emphasis on investment and greater emphasis on consumption. It is also significant that the Soviets seem to be making more use of such capitalistic devices as prices, profits, credit, and interest rates.

An economy's capacity for growth is especially significant to man's quest for security. For many years it was generally believed—and perhaps still is by many people—that the only way for low-income groups to raise their standards of living was through capturing part of the income of those who earned more. This is the "share the wealth" idea that was so prevalent

[2] Despite its shortcomings, the annual increase in real gross national product (the dollar value of total output, adjusted for price changes) will be used as a measure of economic growth. These shortcomings are perhaps outweighed by the simplicity of the concept and its wide acceptability as a measure of growth.

[3] The comparisons of U.S. and Soviet growth rates of a few years back were misleading and unduly alarming for several reasons. For one thing, Soviet data are highly questionable, whereas figures for the U.S. economy are comprehensive and carefully prepared. In addition, percentage rates of growth for any short period can be very misleading when used to compare magnitudes as greatly different in size as the U.S. and Soviet economies. Most important is the fact that the Soviet economy is a curious mixture of modern technology in industry and extreme backwardness in agriculture. This means that the transfer of a worker from agriculture to industry results in a sharp productivity gain.

in the United States in the 1930's and which provided the philosophical underpinning for our highly progressive and, at some levels, almost confiscatory system of personal income taxes. More and more people have come to realize that any reasonable amount of such redistribution would add only a small amount to the incomes of low-income groups.[4]

Much more important is the growing awareness that higher standards of living for lower-income groups do not lie primarily in income redistribution, but rather in achieving a higher individual productivity. This means that all contributors to the productive process can have larger incomes, because total income will be larger, and no one need have less. Moreover, a growing, wealthy economy will be much better able to meet (perhaps increasingly through nongovernment channels) the needs of those who are unable to contribute fully to the productive process because of health or other reasons.

Clearly the capacity for economic growth is of vital importance in any society's search for economic security. This importance is driven home by the impact of the five years of uninterrupted growth enjoyed by the U.S. economy beginning in 1961. The factors underlying this growth, along with the outlook for its continuation, are of especial significance to this discussion. I shall return to this question after a few comments on the final criterion for judging economic performance.

Stability. A stable economy can be defined as one in which total output expands at a rate close to that permitted by technology and the availability of labor and equipment; in which useful employment opportunities exist for those persons able, willing, and seeking to work; and in which the over-all level of prices, but not necessarily individual prices, remains about the same. In a market economy, deviations from these conditions of stability have exhibited cyclical characteristics. The

---

[4] For example, if that portion of any family's annual income in excess of $20,000 were reallocated to families with incomes of less than $20,000, the income of the latter would rise by less than $600. This is assuming, of course, that such drastic redistribution could be effected without reducing the total of national income, which would be highly unlikely.

characteristics of the deviations, although certainly not identical within each cycle, have been similar, and the lengths of the cycles have also been similar.

The market economy may rate high marks for efficiency, equity, and growth, but its record with respect to stability is poor. This is especially true of the United States economy. According to the National Bureau of Economic Research, the U.S. economy has experienced twenty-six complete business cycles since 1854. During these cycles, unemployment fluctuated from a minimal level to as high as 25 per cent of the labor force. Over the whole period, prices increased approximately 170 per cent. Clearly this is not a good record.[5]

And it is a record which is of crucial importance to the people of the United States in their quest for economic security. Not only do high levels of unemployment mean a lack of security for the unemployed themselves, but such conditions, if they persist, can strike at the very viability of the market economy itself by leading to drastic changes in political and economic organization. Persistence of high levels of unemployment among youth and among minority groups can also have significant consequences, social and political as well as economic.

Instability impedes man's quest for security in a more fundamental way by slowing economic growth. An economy which expands by a steady, sustainable rate, year in and year out, will tend to grow more over a long period of years than one subjected to recurrent recessions. This is true even though the recessions may be relatively mild and brief (as was the case with the four recessions in the United States between 1946 and 1961). The growth rate is by definition negative during a recession, and the ground that is then lost cannot be wholly made up during a

[5] U.S. Department of Commerce, *Business Cycle Developments* (July 1965), p. 67; U.S. Department of Commerce, *Historical Statistics of the United States, Colonial Times to 1957*, p. 73 (unemployment series begins in 1900); U.S. Department of Commerce, *Historical Statistics of the United States 1789–1945*, pp. 233–34; Joint Economic Committee, *1964 Supplement to Economic Indicators*, p. 95.

period of expansion without endangering its sustainability and thereby bringing on still another contraction. Moreover, the rate of investment in new plant and equipment tends to slump in recessions. In the long run, it is this rate which is the most important factor in promoting economic growth.

Considerations such as these convince me that the key to a high rate of economic growth in the long run lies in the minimization of recessions in the short run. United States experience in the past five years strongly supports this view. No recessions have occurred; expansion has been almost uninterrupted. Between the final quarters of 1960 and 1965, real gross national product increased at an annual rate of 5.24 per cent, a rate which if sustained would result in a doubling of output every fourteen years. This contrasts with a doubling of output every twenty-one years in the seventy years from 1889 to 1959.

In part, the rapid noninflationary growth of the past five years was made possible by a large supply of unemployed workers and idle machines which could be drawn into active production. But that isn't the whole story. Most significant is the fact that the growth rate has continued at a sustained high level, without outright inflation, during what would normally have been a period of either slow advance or actual decline.

Five years is a very short period in the annals of economic history. It would therefore be quite premature to conclude that the United States has solved all the problems of avoiding economic instability, thereby assuring high and sustained economic growth and thus greatly aiding man's search for security. The odds are strongly in favor of additional contractions in business activity as time goes by. But the highly favorable experience of 1961–1965 supports the view that we should and can do better in the future than in the past, and it is therefore appropriate to examine this recent experience to see what lessons can be distilled for future actions.

It is this examination, which can be highly illuminating with respect to man's quest for security, with which the remainder of this paper is concerned.

The United States Economy in the 1960's: Lessons of the Experience

To say that U.S. economic performance thus far in the 1960's has been very good indeed is not to say that it has been perfect. For one thing, a chronic deficit in this nation's international transactions has plagued government policy-makers. A program of voluntary restraint in foreign lending and investing established early in 1965 resulted in an immediate sharp decline in the deficit, but it is too early to say whether this improvement can be sustained, or whether the voluntary program itself can be maintained for very long.

Discussion of the balance of payments problem is beyond the scope of this paper. This is definitely *not* to say that the problem is of little importance to the achievement of sustained economic growth, for failure to deal effectively with it could undermine economic prosperity not only in the United States, but in other free world nations as well. The remainder of my remarks are, therefore, based on the assumption that true equilibrium in the U.S. balance of payments will be restored and maintained.[6]

Another problem is unemployment, which many observers believe has been too high throughout the entire expansion of the 1960's. The rate remained above 5 per cent during most of the period and only recently fell below 4.5 per cent, still about .5 of one percentage point above the administration's so-called interim goal.

I shall have more to say about the unemployment problem, and especially its relation to the sustained expansion of the past five years. First, however, I would like to discuss the four factors that seem to me to account primarily for this highly favorable performance. They are: (1) the fundamental sources of economic strength in a free-choice, market economy; (2) federal tax

[6] For comments on the nature and gravity of the balance of payments problem, see my testimony before the Subcommittee on International Finance of the Senate Committee on Banking and Currency on March 25, 1965, pp. 545–585, and the resolutions of the American Bankers Association adopted at its 91st Annual Convention, October 6, 1965, *Report of the Resolutions Comittee*, pp. 8–10.

policies; (3) Federal Reserve monetary policies; and (4) stability in unit labor costs.

Strength of the Market Economy. The U.S. market economy has performed very well during the entire period since World War II, but especially so during the 1960's. To contrast the two experiences, one need only recall that twenty years after the First World War we were still struggling to emerge from the Great Depression which had begun nearly ten years earlier. One worker out of five was unemployed. In this instance, the drastic postwar deflation which many people feared has been avoided, and the four postwar recessions have been mild and short-lived.

The experience of the past five years is even more favorable. The purpose here is not, however, to recount the statistics, but to emphasize instead that, in contrast to views in the 1930's, the market economy as it operates in the United States has unquestionably demonstrated its strength and adaptability. Without doubt, federal economic policies have helped achieve this record, but the major share of the credit must be given to the characteristics of the market economy itself, especially its emphasis on private initiative, freedom of choice, and competitive pricing.

It is the individual United States citizen who, as a consumer, was primarily responsible for the nation's not sliding into recession when a slump threatened in 1962. If a recession had then occurred, the expansion would have ended after only sixteen to eighteen months, and would have been recorded as one of the shortest ones of history.

To understand the events of that period, and especially to comprehend the important role played by the American consumer, one must think back to the circumstances existing when John F. Kennedy became President of the United States in January, 1961. At that time the economy was just emerging from the fourth postwar recession, a slump so mild that real gross national product fell only for a couple of quarters and on an annual basis did not decline at all.

The business community did not trust the Kennedy administration. The roots of this distrust were deep, some growing out of the Democratic party's strong labor orientation and some growing out of both the Roosevelt and the Truman administrations' seeming disregard of sustained business investment and adequate profits as factors vital to the health of a market economy. Moreover, the Democratic platform of 1960 was disturbing to many businessmen; they believed it called for higher and higher federal spending and easier and easier monetary conditions—a combination which, in their view, could only lead to inflation and a collapse of the dollar in international markets. In this respect, it is important to recall that the gold outflow swelled to huge proportions in the latter part of 1960.

In view of this background, businessmen awaited the early actions of the new administration with considerable misgiving. When one of its earliest actions was an attempt to change the long-established procedures followed by the Business Advisory Council (consisting mainly of heads of major U.S. corporations) in its meetings with government officials, many felt that their misgivings had indeed been justified. Couple these developments with what businessmen believed to be vigorous enforcement of the antitrust laws by the new President's brother—a happenstance that added a personal flavor to the actions—and it is not surprising that many business leaders concluded that business was in for at least four and perhaps eight years of "persecution" from Washington.

Business leaders were wrong, and they were exceedingly myopic in not seeing the handwriting on the wall in the early days of the Kennedy administration. This handwriting was in the form of its tax policies and was first evident in a legislative proposal for a tax credit for business investment in new equipment. This concern with business investment, which was an implicit recognition of the role of adequate profits in a market economy, stood in sharp contrast to the philosophy of the Roosevelt and Truman administrations.

The business community did not support the investment credit, even though business leaders have since embraced it. Some viewed it as a gimmick that, if enacted, would probably postpone the day of the badly needed reductions in unduly high corporate and individual tax rates. Organized labor also was very much against the credit. The administration was in the ironical position of having to push for its passage over the objections of both labor and business![7]

The views of the administration with respect to the importance of business investment were further indicated by the revisions of the Internal Revenue Service guidelines relating to depreciable assets (Bulletin F). These investment-inducing revisions, work on which was initiated in the Eisenhower administration, were issued in 1961 and 1962.

Just as business leaders were beginning to read and welcome the signs pointing to pragmatic rather than doctrinaire economic policies on the part of the Kennedy administration, the famous steel price incident of April, 1962, all but destroyed the emerging rapport. If businessmen view anything as sacred, it's the authority to establish pricing policies in response to market pressures; and the heads of several steel companies had evidently come to the conclusion that market forces called for higher prices.

President Kennedy, on the other hand, believed that a major steel company settlement with the labor unions, which had just been completed, involved an implied commitment on the part of the companies *not* to raise prices. The President's anger and actions on hearing of the action by the steel companies in announcing price increases are a matter of record: he mobilized executive power as perhaps it had never before been mobilized in peacetime. The price increases were rescinded.

The President's victory almost turned out to be Pyrrhic. Business distrust of the administration mounted, and this lack of confidence was translated into more tangible evidence of economic trouble. In late May, the stock market, reacting at least in part to the awesome show of presidential power and its use to coerce market decisions, underwent an exceedingly sharp decline. More important, however, was the subsequent slump in business investment in new plant and equipment. This decline could well have triggered a recession; and, in retrospect, it is

[7] Leaders of the American Bankers Association endorsed the investment credit at an early date as a highly desirable, albeit selective, reduction in the tax rate on business profits.

surprising that it did not. Although it is impossible to say how much of the decline can be attributed to the concern of businessmen with the economic policies of the administration—and, in particular, the willingness to use presidential power to shape market decisions—the stability of interest rates and business profits, coupled with the strength of consumer demand at that time,—all suggest that fear of administration policies was the major factor.

That a recession did not occur—total output moved upward with hardly a pause—can be attributed primarily to two factors, both of which emphasize the fundamental strength of our market economy. The first is the dependability of the American consumer, whose continued spending for goods and services made up in large part for the decline in business investment. The second is the tax policy of the Kennedy administration, which emerged in full form in late 1962 and early 1963, and which even in prospect added strength to the economy and helped avoid imminent recession. Tax reductions, which were the major substance of the Kennedy tax programs, imply greater reliance on the private sector than on government for stimulating economic growth and progress. In contrast with increased government spending, tax cuts emphasize decisions by individuals and businesses to spend and invest.

The reliance on tax cuts as opposed to further increases in federal spending to stimulate the economy may have been a gamble on the part of the Kennedy administration, but if so, it was a most worthy and successful one.

Federal Tax Policies for Economic Growth. In terms of current income levels, the Kennedy-Johnson administrations have reduced the federal tax bill by upwards of twenty billion dollars, but federal revenues are today higher than when the first reductions went into effect. Paradoxical? Not when it is realized that the U.S. economy has for too long been suffering from a tax system conceived in depression and shaped further in war—a tax system badly suited to the needs of the 1960's.

The tax system, which had its origin in the 1930's, and whose major form still persists, weighs heavily against individual initiative, business investment, and profits. The corporate tax, by reducing by almost one-half the after-tax return of most corporate investments, discourages new ventures and expansion by business firms. The high marginal rates on individual incomes discourage effort but raise little revenue. Such a tax system might be viewed as logical by those who want to soak the big corporations and the wealthy, and might also be quite suitable in a wartime inflationary economy, but it has little justification in the U.S. economy of the 1960's.

The U.S. tax system has in fact been acting as a drag on the market economy. It is not surprising that the four major tax actions of the Kennedy-Johnson administrations—the revision of Bulletin F (1961 and 1962), the investment credit (1962), the federal income tax cut (1964), and the federal excise tax cut (1965)—have served to stimulate the economy; and, as a result, economic activity has advanced. The expansive impact on federal revenues, which are geared closely to the level of economic activity, more than offsets the contractive impact of the reductions in tax rates. Consequently, total federal revenues have increased.

But it is easy to read the wrong lessons from the tax cuts of 1961-1965. If we do, future tax policies may err, and the sustainability of future expansions may be impaired. The fundamental factor to be recognized is not that just *any* tax cut will help maintain balanced economic expansion. There is also danger that too much may be expected of federal fiscal policies, of which tax policy is perhaps the most important component.

It is tempting to conclude that the impact of a tax cut that releases, say, one billion dollars would be the same as any other that released the same amount; the logic for this conclusion is based on a simple aggregative demand approach to income determination that assumes any increase in after-tax incomes will result in a given impact on gross national spending. But such an approach overlooks the dynamic and forceful role played by investment in a market economy. Economists have long recognized that, given the strength of final demand, an increase in the rate of return on new investment in plant and equipment tends to increase the pace of investment. A cut in the tax rate on business profits is a simple and direct way of raising that return.

The higher investment spending induced by a reduction in profits taxes has important economic effects of both a short-run and a long-run nature. In the short run, the increase in investment spending is in itself an increase in demand for goods and services and thereby bolsters income; the so-called "multiplier effect" extends the impact further in time and amount. In the long run, this higher investment spending helps raise the rate of economic growth by adding to the stock of productive equipment.

In my judgment, under the conditions existing and likely to exist in the 1960's, cuts in business taxes will stimulate demand more strongly than cuts in individual income taxes. Admittedly, this cannot now be proved, but the first tentative analyses of the 1964 income tax cut support the conclusion.[8]

This is by no means to say that further cuts in personal income taxes should be avoided; such cuts can help bolster effective demand and also provide a useful means for helping to

[8] See, for example, the speech by Arthur M. Okun, a member of the President's Council of Economic Advisers, before the American Statistical Association, Philadelphia, Pa., September 10, 1965. On the basis of econometric analysis, Okun estimated that the thirteen-billion-dollar cut in taxes would ultimately result in a thirty-six-billion-dollar increment in gross national product, and that the so-called multiplier for the personal tax cut was about 2.6 times and for the corporate cut about 3.4 times. He pointed out that the corporate multiplier might, for certain technical reasons, be biased on the high side (that is, would actually be less than 3.4). On the other hand, his analysis did not take into account the expectational effects of the corporate cut on business investment, which probably began to be felt a year or so before the reduction was finally passed. As noted earlier, I believe that those expectational effects were quite important, and helped greatly to avoid a premature snuffing out of the expansion in 1962 and 1963.

It should be noted that Okun's analysis has not gone unchallenged, although the attack was not on the basis of the relative impact of personal versus corporate tax cuts. See the comments of David Meiselman on Okun's paper, delivered at the same meeting.

spread the fruits of an expanding economy widely among the people. Cuts in upper-bracket rates can be justified because the marginal rates ranging as high as 70 per cent dull incentive and, in any event, contribute little to revenue. As for the lower brackets, the personal income tax structure is at its most progressive slope at that point between the payment of no tax and the first bracket.[9] Further improvement in this area can and should be achieved as economic conditions warrant, but it must be recognized that small cuts in the lower brackets involve very large amounts of revenue.

Thus the case is still strong for broadly based tax reduction as economic conditions permit. Moreover, viewed solely from a political point of view, broadly based reduction—affecting business as well as both low- and high-income-bracket individuals—will gain the greatest support in Congress. It is fortunate that, for once at least, political and economic forces run parallel and are not in conflict.

In one sense, the growth-inhibiting tax structure which the United States economy inherited from the 1930's and 1940's is a blessing, in that it readily lends itself to further improvement which can serve to strengthen the forces of economic expansion whenever necessary. But there are two important dangers that should be noted.

Economic conditions in late 1965 are far different from those in early 1961. In early 1961 unemployment amounted to 7 per cent of the labor force and industrial capacity was being utilized at a rate of only 77 per cent. Clearly the economy was in need of stimulation, and the tax cuts effected by the Kennedy-Johnson administrations were well suited to the task.

Today, however, unemployment has declined below 4.5 per cent of the labor force and is much lower with respect to married men and skilled workers. Industrial capacity is now being utilized at a rate estimated to be close to 90 per cent, only slightly below what many observers believe to be the most

---

[9] See the comments of Douglas Dillon, then Secretary of the Treasury, at the American Bankers Association Symposium on Federal Taxation, February 1965, *Proceedings*, pp. 3–10.

desirable level. The danger is clear: the economy's low margin of unused resources and qualified labor is such that further tax cuts at this time would run the serious risk of producing outright inflation. Such inflation would both weaken our balance of payments position and seriously threaten the sustainability of the economic advance. This is especially true in view of what may be a sharp increase in federal spending resulting from intensification of our war effort in Vietnam.

Federal tax cuts, therefore, should not be looked upon as a way of life; they possess an inherent inflationary potential which is especially marked when the margin of unutilized labor and productive facilities is small. Still, it is reassuring that the existing tax structure contains a large margin of expansive potential which, if spread prudently over the next decade or so, can serve greatly the cause of sustained economic growth.

Another danger is that the success of recent tax policies in promoting growth may lead policy-makers to conclude that federal fiscal policies can now be utilized easily and effectively to avoid *all* deviations from a steady growth line. This view is part of what journalists have referred to as the "new economics," and some would have us believe that Washington policy-makers embrace it wholeheartedly.

This part of the "new economics" is not really new; it is in reality a version of the compensatory fiscal policies which economists have long discussed—that the fiscal policies of the federal government (relating to taxing and spending) can serve as a delicate and constantly used balance wheel for the enterprise economy.

Here is how the approach would work in theory. On the basis of projections of public and private spending, an estimate would be reached as to the accompanying level of unemployment. If projections showed that unemployment would be too high, federal spending would be raised and/or taxes reduced by an amount just sufficient to raise total spending and pull unemployment down to the desired level. If projections showed that unemployment would be too low, thus resulting in inflationary pressures, federal fiscal policies would be finely adjusted to the opposite end; that is, spending would be reduced and/or taxes raised just enough to dampen total public and private spending and remove the inflationary stimulus of overfull employment. To facilitate these fine adjustments, Congress would be asked to give the President some power, perhaps closely circumscribed, to raise or lower income tax rates on his own prerogative.[10]

This approach seems to me to expect too much of federal fiscal policies. The council itself warns that its concept of the full employment surplus "cannot measure perfectly the effect of a given budgetary change because it does not reflect changes in the composition of the budget. Moreover, a rise in the level of the budget may have a stimulating effect even with no change in the full employment surplus."[11]

A much more important objection relates to the need for great accuracy in economic forecasting, especially under current circumstances in which changes in tax rates and spending must go through a difficult and uncertain legislative process. It would be one thing if we could foresee with reasonable certainty the course of the economy a year or so in advance; under such circumstances the finely tuned applications of a fully compensatory fiscal policy might perhaps be implemented successfully. But the inherent lags involved in moving the federal fiscal apparatus, coupled with a highly unsatisfactory record of forecasting (on the part of both private as well as government economists), lead me to question strongly whether federal

---

[10] The Council of Economic Advisers speaks of a "full employment surplus or deficit," which is the relationship between federal spending and revenues (on a national income account basis) at the full employment level. "Changes in this surplus indicate whether the Federal budget is becoming more or less expansive. When aggregate demand needs a stimulus in order to achieve full employment, it is appropriate to reduce the full-employment surplus. When a restrictive influence is called for, the full-employment surplus should be raised." See the council's *Annual Report for 1965*, pp. 63, 97.

[11] *Ibid.*, p. 63.

stabilization policy should be aimed at straightening out almost every wiggle of the business cycle.[12]

This view is not contradicted by the experience with federal tax policies in 1961–1965; in fact, experience with the massive income tax cut of 1964 reinforces it. Federal economic planners had actually hoped to have the cut go into effect almost a year earlier than it did, and their forecasts for calendar year 1963 (which turned out to be highly accurate) were based on that assumption. Actually, the economy moved ahead strongly in 1963 without benefit of the tax cut (although anticipatory factors surely helped). Because of the vagaries of politics, which slowed the movement of the tax bill through the Congress, the timing perhaps turned out to be much better than as originally planned.

The summer of 1962 provides a clear-cut example of circumstances in which incorrect forecasting could easily lead to the wrong policies. The preponderance of expert opinion at that time was that the economy was in imminent danger of recession, and there were reports that the Council of Economic Advisers strongly favored an immediate income tax cut to bolster the economy. Congressional leaders balked, however, and President Kennedy had to be content with telling the American people that he would come to the Congress in January, 1963, with a proposal for a major income tax cut. I was one who believed that we were moving into recession at that time. But on the basis of hindsight, I have to admit that a quick income tax cut then—some eighteen months in advance of when it actually took place—would have been inadvisable.

These events are not recounted in criticism of government policy-makers, but to emphasize that our knowledge and techniques are not yet sufficient to provide a basis for the type of

---

[12] Enactment of legislation giving the President the power to vary federal income tax rates, even if it could be effected, would provide only a partial answer to this objection. Forecasting would still be necessary. In addition, the political difficulties inherent in reducing spending and/or raising taxes when inflation threatens should not be underestimated.

forecasting required by the fiscal policy of the "new economics." But this does not imply that fiscal policy has no role to play. As emphasized earlier, the existing tax structure is so badly suited to the environment of the 1960's—is so inhibiting to sustained economic growth—that we are fortunate in having considerable leeway for fostering future expansion by gradually reducing the tax burden. But tax policies of this type should not be viewed as delicately wielded instruments to eliminate all business cycle fluctuations. Rather, each reduction, carried out when economic slack begins to emerge, would be a step toward the long-run goal of reducing the drag on the enterprise system that results from our archaic tax structure.[13]

Such policies can pay especially rich dividends to the American people in their search for economic security—in spreading the fruits of current growth and also in fostering further growth. Inflationary dangers can be minimized if the cuts are effected only under appropriate conditions. And, in any event, the powerful stabilizing tool of monetary policy can be brought into play.

Expansive Monetary Policy in the 1960's. A steadily expansive monetary policy is the third factor that contributed to the sustainability of the business expansion of the 1960's. The expansiveness of monetary policy is demonstrated by almost any measure: the growth of demand and time deposits in commercial banks; the expansion in savings accounts and other liquid assets; and, in the face of rising credit demands, stability of long-term interest rates (although short-term money market rates have been allowed to rise in response to balance of

[13] To argue for reform of our archaic tax structure by reducing rates is not to endorse a long string of deficits in the federal budget. To embrace such deficits as a way of fiscal life would inhibit efforts to achieve economy and efficiency in government as well as remove an important barrier against the development of an ever larger and more powerful federal government. But it is important to understand that our archaic and depressive tax system is a major obstruction in the way of balancing the federal budget, because of its impact on economic activity and federal revenues. The upsurge in revenues in response to the tax cuts of recent years supports this view.

payments pressures) and stability in bank lending rates, which only recently have begun to increase significantly in response to a record-breaking growth in bank loans.

To say that monetary policy has helped fire the expansion is not to say that it has been noncontroversial. Many academicians maintain that monetary policy has not been expansive enough. They argue that, because of the balance of payments problem, monetary policy has not been permitted to make its full contribution to reducing unemployment to the interim goal of 4 per cent. Presumably they would have favored the extreme monetary ease that was achieved in the postwar recessions of 1954 and 1958. Other observers disagree, averring that monetary policy has been excessively expansive and has thereby prevented us from arriving at a fundamental solution to our balance of payments problem.

I find myself approximately in the middle of these two groups. I am convinced that monetary policy would have been easier in the absence of the balance of payments problem; an easier policy would probably have promoted a somewhat higher level of total demand and helped bring unemployment to a lower level. But this does not mean that such policies would have been desirable even if viewed solely from a domestic standpoint. This is because a more expansive monetary policy could easily have created imbalances in the economic expansion which would have threatened its sustainability and shortened its duration.

Stated differently, it is my judgment that a "crash program" of expansive measures to restore a very low level of unemployment by, say, the end of 1963 would have run serious risks; unemployment might have temporarily been pushed down, but an economic downturn might well have occurred shortly thereafter. This judgment is supported by experience in the postwar business cycles. It is also supported by developments at the time of this writing, in October, 1965, when inflationary pressures are clearly mounting with unemployment still running close to 4.5 per cent of the labor force and some margin of unused capacity still existing. The real question is how low aggregate unemployment can be pushed without resulting in strong pressures on costs and prices. My own view is that we are very close to that point at the present time.

Looking to the future, it should be clear that monetary policy should continue to play a vital role along with fiscal policy as an important stabilization device. In this respect, it is important to recognize that strongly expansive monetary policies cannot be justified at all times and under all conditions. Indeed, one of the fundamental purposes of the big income tax cut of 1964 was to create conditions of aggregate demand so strong as to justify the use of a more restrictive monetary policy, thereby helping to reduce our chronic balance of payments deficit. These conditions are now being achieved.

In the long run, flexibility in administration of monetary policy will be especially important as we move toward the achievement of an income tax structure more suited to the needs of our dynamic economy. We cannot expect to time each tax reduction so as to have it fit perfectly with emerging conditions, and we must therefore be ready to use monetary policy flexibly, especially if the economy shows signs of overheating. To the extent the economy can, through an expansive tax policy, be kept close to this point, the better monetary policy can be adjusted to balance of payments problems.

Stability in Unit Labor Costs. Stability in unit labor costs of production has been a major factor contributing to the sustainability of the economic expansion of the 1960's. This stability is in sharp contrast to earlier expansions and helps account both for the near stability of industrial prices and the maintenance of satisfactory profit margins in manufacturing and other industries. Stable prices have in turn helped sustain final demand, both here and abroad, and good profit margins combined with cuts in the tax rate on profits have encouraged businesses to invest heavily in new plant and equipment. This is a thumbnail sketch of how a market economy can and should perform when expectations are stable and public policy is soundly conceived and implemented.

To say that unit labor costs have been remarkably stable is also to say that total labor compensation has risen about equally with productivity. But to observe this truism is not to provide an answer to the crucial question: Why has such stability prevailed in this instance?

Some insight into this important matter can be gained, first, by noting that in the 1961-1965 expansion productivity has risen faster and labor compensation slower than in earlier postwar expansions. In the years 1960-1964, according to the Council of Economic Advisers, gains in output per man hour averaged 3.5 per cent per year, as contrasted with only 2.5 in 1953-1957 and 2.7 in 1957-1960. On the other hand, hourly compensation during the current expansion rose about 3.6 per cent per year, as compared with 4.5 in 1953-1957 and 3.9 in 1957-1960.[14]

One can speculate at length as to why productivity has advanced faster in this expansion than earlier. My own view is that the favorable climate for investment (and in this respect I would place great emphasis on the investment credit, the revision of Bulletin F, and the corporate tax cut) was a major factor encouraging businesses to invest heavily in cost-reducing projects.

As to the slower rate of growth in labor compensation, credit must be shared by the spotlight that has been thrown on national wage settlements by administration sponsorship of the wage-price guideposts, and the avoidance (until recently, at least) of a level of final demand so strong as to put strong pressure on wages and prices.[15]

[14] Council of Economic Advisers, *Annual Report for 1965*, p. 67.

[15] As a general guide for noninflationary wage behavior, the Council of Economic Advisers states that the rate of increase in wage rates in each industry should be equal to the trend rate of productivity change in the economy as a whole. With respect to noninflationary price behavior, the council calls for price reductions if an industry's rate of productivity increase is above the over-all rate, price increases if below, and no change if its productivity trend coincides with the national average.

The council's delineation of the guideposts, along with the evolution of its thinking on the subject, can be found in its 1962 *Report*, pp. 185-190; in its 1963 *Report*, pp. 84-88; in its 1964 *Report*, pp. 118-120; and in its 1965 *Report*, pp. 108-110.

Of the two factors, it is my opinion that the latter—the steady but not excessive growth in final demand—has been by far the more important. This again is a judgment that cannot now be proved, but the recent emergence of stronger cost and price pressures as total output has moved closer to capacity and as unemployment has fallen seem to me strongly to support the view. But even if my view is correct, it does not necessarily follow that the attainment of steady and sustainable economic expansion, as in the first half of the 1960's, requires the maintenance of a reservoir of unemployed labor and equipment at a level higher than we would like to accept. I shall return to this matter in the next section of this paper.

I shall also have more to say about the wage-price guideposts, especially with respect to their appropriateness in a market economy. At this point, it is appropriate to observe that the Council of Economic Advisers itself has refrained from making any strong claims as to their effectiveness. In its 1964 *Report*, the council simply notes that the guideposts have had a "useful influence" and have helped to create "a new climate of opinion."[16]

Regardless of its cause, the stability of unit labor costs during the expansion of the 1960's must be viewed as one of the most important factors contributing to the strength and sustainability of the advance. If, as now appears possible, this stability is being threatened, the sustainability of the advance itself will also be impaired.

A Look Ahead

Viewed in terms of economic performance, how will man's quest for security fare in the U.S. market economy in the years ahead? If one thing stands out in the review of recent experience just presented, it is that the economy undoubtedly possesses the

[16] See pp. 58–59. It should be noted, however, that the council's comments were written *after* the major automobile settlement of September, 1964, which was estimated to have been about twice the amount suggested by the wage guidepost, but *before* the steel settlement of a year later, which was very close to the guidepost.

potential for long and sustained periods of economic growth. It is highly doubtful that all recessions can be avoided, but the experience of the 1960's should surely encourage us to strive for a better record than we have attained in the past. And if the number and severity of recessions can be reduced, the dividends in terms of greater growth and prosperity—and, therefore, man's economic security—will be great indeed.

To say that sustained growth is attainable is not to say that it will be attained; this depends upon many factors, some of which are beyond our control. But the soundness of our public policy actions is of vital importance.

The prospects for continued soundness in federal fiscal and monetary policies are favorable, especially so if federal policy-makers read the right lessons from experience thus far in the 1960's. As noted earlier, these lessons seem to me to point toward additional broadly based tax cuts as conditions warrant. However, it would be a big mistake—political, as well as economic—to concentrate such cuts solely in the lower-income brackets; low-bracket cuts are very expensive but stimulate investment only indirectly. In addition, it is tempting but dangerous to conclude that federal fiscal policies can be used to offset every deviation from steady economic growth.

As to monetary policy, the major lesson of the early 1960's seems to me to be that a steadily expansive monetary policy can greatly serve the cause of sustained growth so long as unutilized resources and labor exist in relatively ample amounts. Flexibility in the administration of such policies must, however, be maintained. Depending on the strength of demand and the availability of unused resources, flexibility may require a strongly expansive policy, a moderately expansive policy, or, at times, a strongly restrictive policy.

When I turn to the outlook for stability in labor costs and the prospect for protecting the fundamental sources of strength in our free-choice, market economy, I am less optimistic.

Outlook for Stability in Labor Costs. In its *Annual Report for 1964*, the Council of Economic Advisers states its belief that "the economy could operate at a 4 per cent unemployment rate today without substantial strains on either labor supplies or plant capacity." This statement was subject to question when first published last January; it is open to even more serious challenge today. Even though unemployment is still above the interim goal of 4 per cent, pressures on costs and prices are clearly increasing. The stability of unit labor costs that has meant so much to the strength and duration of the business expansion is in clear danger of disruption.

If this assessment is correct, serious questions must be raised as to whether even the interim unemployment goal of 4 per cent is attainable without serious cost and price pressures—*given the existing level of skills of the labor force and the limited opportunity for training and work that is open to some workers, particularly nonwhites.* I have underlined this qualification because it is of signal importance, pointing the way for reconciling what may now be irreconcilable goals of full employment (if defined as 4 per cent or below) and sustainable economic growth.

One need not be drawn into the continuing argument among economists as to whether so-called structural unemployment has increased in recent years to conclude that our major route toward solution of the existing unemployment problem lies in attacking what may be viewed as structural factors. Otherwise, we would not be plagued with such high unemployment rates among the unskilled and poorly educated, among youth, and among minority groups. As noted earlier, unemployment among married men is ranging only slightly above 2 per cent; seasoned and skilled workers are in very short supply. In contrast, unemployment among teen-agers is approximately three times the over-all rate. The jobless rate for nonwhites is almost twice the rate for white workers.

There is no simple answer to this problem. Some economists believe that lack of sufficient spread between the wages of skilled and unskilled workers—seasoned workers versus youngsters just entering the labor force—is an important contributing factor.[17]

[17] See, for example, George H. Hildebrand, "Structural Unemployment and Cost-Push Inflation in the United States," a paper presented to the American Bankers Association Conference of University Professors, Purdue University, August 1965. The full proceedings of this conference are to be published in 1966 by Richard D. Irwin, Inc.

This view seems to me to have considerable merit; surely the lack of adequate wage differentials would encourage employers to avoid hiring unskilled workers and training them. It is accordingly most disturbing to witness proposals which would reduce the spread still further, such as the current proposal to increase the level and coverage of the federal minimum wage. Congress should indeed think twice before taking actions which, although ostensibly in labor's benefit, may complicate further the task of reducing unacceptably high unemployment rates among unskilled workers.

In fact, if we are really serious about reducing hard-core unemployment, we probably should be considering reductions, not increases, in the federal minimum wage for certain occupations and in certain areas. To make this suggestion is to risk being tarred as an eighteenth-century reactionary. I like to think of myself rather as a citizen and economist genuinely concerned with the problem of finding jobs for the millions of young people who will be entering the labor force in the years ahead. These young people deserve a chance to make their own way— a chance they may not get if a clumsy federal statute, however well intentioned, prices them out of the market from the very start.

It has become almost trite to say that the fundamental attack on the heart of the unemployment problem lies in education, training, and increased opportunities for unskilled and minority-group workers. But, trite as the words may be, this is still the most promising—indeed, indispensable—approach. A start has been made in this direction through federal legislation enacted in recent years. But it does not follow that it is solely or even principally up to the federal government to deal with this problem. In fact, the admittedly brief experience with the federal antipoverty program indicates that projects in which the federal government acts only as starter and catalyst but which rely primarily on local initiative and local effort fare the best. Stated differently, both business and what Richard Cornuelle calls the "independent sector" have important and perhaps vital roles to play in eliminating hard-core unemployment through education, training, and the removal of discrimination.[18]

If these efforts are not successful, the pressures for pushing unemployment lower and lower by stimulating aggregate demand will continue strong. If yielded to, the resulting rupture of the cost-price stability which has meant so much to the business advance can take a far greater toll in unemployment and lost output than exists today. I have no doubt that indefinite continuation of strongly expansive fiscal and monetary policies can push unemployment down a few more notches. But I am just as firmly convinced that the cost-price pressures which will be induced will ultimately lead to recession, with rising unemployment of both men and equipment. If so, the victory of achieving some temporary reduction in the too high level of unemployment will have been Pyrrhic indeed.

Guideposts, Guidelines, and the Market Economy. As noted earlier, the Kennedy administration in 1962 presented a set of wage-price guideposts designed to point the way to non-inflationary wage and price behavior. In 1965 the Johnson administration enunciated a set of guidelines for foreign lending and investing by U.S. banks and corporations. The issue here is not the effectiveness of such programs, but their appropriateness as permanent appendages to a market economy.[19] In view

[18] See Richard Cornuelle, *Reclaiming the American Dream* (New York: Random House, 1965), especially pp. 31–34. My remarks have been confined to the future performance of our economic system. Cornuelle's book—one of the most significant works to come forth since the Second World War—is highly relevant to the future performance of *both* our political and economic systems. It is at the same time a manifesto and a call to arms for conservatives, charting the way for those of us who are convinced that such problems as poverty, hard-core unemployment, and juvenile crime will not go away, and deserve concentrated attention, but who are fearful of the stultifying impact of an ever larger federal establishment. Cornuelle's book, for the first time, shows us how to react to these problems in a positive rather than a negative manner. It is *must* reading for every thoughtful American, conservative and liberal alike.

[19] Elsewhere I have severely criticized the wage-price guideposts in terms of effectiveness. See my remarks before the 14th Annual Business Conference of the School of Business, Rutgers, the State University, New

of the gravity and immediacy of the balance of payments problem, I do not question the need for use of the voluntary program until permanent corrective measures can be put into effect; banks have cooperated fully with the program and will continue to do so.

The fundamental danger of guideposts and guidelines as permanent devices for influencing crucial decisions in a market economy is that proliferation of such programs can seriously undermine the very strength of the economy itself. The market system's reliance on private initiative, self-interest, the profit motive, and competitive pricing provides the fundamental strength and drive of the system. Guideposts and guidelines, however, rely on public opinion and patriotism—and under circumstances such as the steel-price incident of 1962, executive power—to induce market participants to behave in ways other than they would behave if reacting solely to market pressures and in the best interests of those whom they represent. I am not referring here to short-run self-interest, but to long-run, enlightened self-interest.

Guideposts and guidelines, if effectively implemented, are only a step away from the direct controls which are used in centralized economies but have been tolerated by the people of the United States only in war. Indeed, it can be argued that the

---

Brunswick, N.J., May 8, 1962 (reprinted in *Vital Speeches* [June 1962], pp. 530–533), and my comments before the American Bankers Association Symposium on Employment, Washington, D.C., Feb. 24, 1964 (*Proceedings*, pp. 102–118). For other critical comments, see the remarks of Professor John Dunlop at the same symposium (*Ibid.*, pp. 86–88); *The Morgan Guaranty Survey*, October 1964, pp. 3–10; and Arthur F. Burns, "Wages and Prices by Formula?" *Harvard Business Review* (March-April 1965), pp. 55–64.

A sizable body of academic opinion—although not necessarily a majority—endorses an approach similar to that embodied in the guideposts. See, for example, the remarks of Professor Henry C. Wallich at the A.B.A. Symposium (*Proceedings*, pp. 67–77). Professor Hildebrand, quoted earlier, also believes that we must rely heavily on the guideposts to keep wage increases in line with productivity gains.

voluntary guidepost or guideline approach—if continued for a protracted period extending beyond a short-run emergency—is even more objectionable than wage, price, and lending-investment controls openly administered by a government board. Such approaches may work the will of government in a market economy without benefit of the mandate of the people obtained through congressional debate and action.

Credit guidelines may have a place as temporary emergency measures. But even if meant to be temporary, substantial dangers exist. If the measures work, they work not in the manner of market processes but in the manner of direct controls. If the measures do not work, and if unsatisfactory conditions persist, it is only natural to turn to a stiffer "voluntary" program or perhaps even direct controls.

Still, with vigilance and care, such approaches can play a useful temporary role in our type of market economy. But it cannot be emphasized too heavily that they are no substitute for fundamental correctives. This is especially true with respect to restoring fundamental equilibrium to the U.S. balance of payments.[20]

The wage-price guideposts are also substitutes for market processes which fail to promote noninflationary wage settlements—settlements which result in average wage increases no

[20] I stated earlier that I would not discuss the solution to this problem in this paper, but simply assume that such equilibrium would be restored. Perhaps this is not quite fair, and I should perhaps add that experience has demonstrated that attack on only one or a limited number of sectors of balance of payments problems often proves fruitless. The need is for an intensified across-the-board effort. At the present time, domestic conditions would support some additional firming of monetary policy, and this might greatly help our balance of payments position. In addition, the outflow of dollars connected with our foreign aid and military programs continues to be quite large, and the latter is likely to rise further as a result of the Vietnam situation. It seems to me that the time has come for a better sharing of the costs of Free World defense among Free World nations—a change which could sharply reduce the foreign exchange costs of our military program. Similar observations can be made about our foreign aid program.

greater than increases in over-all productivity.[21] The reason seems to me to be perfectly clear: unsatisfactory bargaining arrangements between labor and management which force many industries to grant excessive wage increases.

In my judgment, the solution to the problem of achieving noninflationary pricing and wage decisions does not lie in providing for government participation in these decisions, either directly through legislation or indirectly through persuasion. The solution lies in achieving a market balance among bargaining groups which, on the average but not invariably, will result in noninflationary wage and price decisions in response to market forces. Underlying this suggestion, of course, is the assumption that fiscal and monetary policies will help assure the existence of aggregate demand sufficient to offer adequate employment opportunities and a high rate of utilization of industrial capacity, but without encouraging inflationary pressures.

Stated differently, I strongly advocate an approach that works through, not against, market processes and forces—an approach which history clearly has shown is the only viable one in a society of free men and free institutions.

---

[21] I use the word "noninflationary" because it is commonly used for such purposes, but I do not believe that the usage is correct. Its use in this context implies that any wage settlement in excess of national gains in productivity will have inflationary consequences, whereas it seems clear to me that the impact will be basically contractionary in nature. This is because the settlement, unless offset by a greater expansion in fiscal and/or monetary policy than would otherwise have been appropriate, will result either in an investment-shrinking reduction in business profits or a demand-reducing increase in unit prices.

The contractionary impact of such settlements was partly hidden during the postwar period by the presence of accommodating federal policies (and a big cushion of liquidity in the economy which financed higher prices through a rise in the velocity of the money supply). But even though partly hidden, the increases in unit labor costs, as noted earlier, were big factors bringing on the postwar recessions, and cost stability in recent years has helped sustain the current expansion. In the future, international competitiveness will help prevent us from being so extravagant by serving as a strong disciplining factor.

If this approach means the figurative—although perhaps not literal—breaking up of certain national labor unions for bargaining purposes, then so be it. The confrontation every so often of a labor leader, representing many thousands of workers, with a businessman, representing billions of dollars of industrial assets, meeting together to reach agreements (or attempting to reach agreements) affecting the well-being of almost every citizen of the nation, seems to me to have no place in a market economy.

This faulty mechanism can be repaired without doing fundamental damage to labor. In fact, in the long run, labor could well benefit, along with other participants in the market process. For, if my judgments are correct, the continuation of our present arrangements, given our commonly accepted employment goals and the present state of skill and opportunity in the labor force, could only serve to impair the efficient functioning of our market economy. This would hurt all of us, worker and boss alike.

Perhaps it is time that the labor movement, in which a new generation of leaders is beginning to assume power, came to realize that, in the long run, what is good for our highly successful market economy is also good for labor.

Conclusion

I close with a confession. I have never started work on a paper of this type with my concluding remarks clear in my mind. This paper is no exception. I am not referring to the fundamental theses offered here—namely, that the superiority of the market economy in furthering man's quest for security has been proved beyond doubt, and that the future holds good prospects if we but learn and heed the lessons of the past.

But if these are the major conclusions of this paper, surely there is an important subthesis. A number of years ago, a good friend of mine and an astute economist at the Federal Reserve Bank of Philadelphia, Clay J. Anderson, wrote a series of articles for that bank's excellent business review on the general theme of "The Quest for Stability."

The relationship between the quest for stability and the quest for security existed only in my subconscious when I started this paper, but now the relation is clear. A stable market economy provides the best route to man's economic security—not static stability, but the dynamic type that has characterized the United States market economy in the 1960's. This over-all stability hides within its cloak the hard work, innovation, risk-taking, and—sometimes—failure that combine to make a market economy the boon it is in helping meet man's material needs.

This dynamic stability would mean the absence of the recessions that have in the past injured human dignity, through unemployment, and slowed our rate of economic expansion. But experience tells us that this complete dynamic stability, with no recessions, resulting in a steady move upward at a rate of 3 to 5 per cent a year, is unattainable. Or is it?

When I was growing up in a small Texas town in the 1930's, I used to marvel at the exploits of Buck Rogers, but also chuckle to myself because I knew that man—at least during my lifetime—would never reach the moon. Man on the moon is now in sight, because we've learned from past experience. Economic security is still not in sight, but, fundamentally, I think we are on the right track. And opportunities to explore these problems cannot help but move us farther down that track.

Comment by CAMPBELL R. MCCONNELL

One cannot quarrel with Dr. Walker's basic theme that long-run economic growth is the fountainhead of abundance and therefore of great consequence for the economic security of man. But surely this portrayal is grossly incomplete in that economic insecurity—the major manifestation of which is poverty—is in large measure an allocational and distributional problem. I see many compelling reasons for advocating an expanding gross national product, but to deduce that such growth will automatically resolve the twin problems of income inequality and economic insecurity borders on wishful thinking. A comprehensive analysis of economic security must be concerned not only with the size, but also the composition and distribution, of the national output. My basic premise is that the quality and the distribution of national output have as much, if not more, bearing upon the achievement of economic security than does the quantity of output. One might even argue in the extreme that an increase in the national income which is accompanied by greater income disparities between rich and poor could diminish human well-being for society as a whole.[1] More specifically, the market economy's definition of distributional equity which Dr. Walker poses—that in general each participant in the productive process should receive income in precise proportion to his contribution to that process—is flatly unacceptable to me. Indeed, is it not true that the viability and acceptability of the capitalistic system has been enhanced by public

[1] See Walter A. Weisskopf, "Economic Growth and Human Well-Being," *Quarterly Review of Economics and Business*, Summer 1964, pp. 17–29.

policies designed to alter the amoral distribution of income which the market economy provides?

But let me state my position more positively. Achievement of the high long-term growth rate advocated by Dr. Walker—that is, the persistent drive toward an opulent society—fosters two closely related tendencies which in my judgment pose serious obstacles to the more complete realization of economic security. In the first place, the abundant economy, virtually by definition, is a highly complex, highly interdependent, and highly dynamic society. It entails an environment in which the individual or family has less and less control over its economic fate and security. Technological progress, rapid and unpredictable shifts in consumer demand, changes in the rate of growth, and, I might add, errors in forecasting or judgment on the part of monetary and fiscal authorities, can generate sources of insecurity for which most individuals and many businesses have no adequate defense. In the opulent society the individual is no longer the architect of his own economic security. A second and not unrelated tendency is this: the course of economic events—the increasing affluence of society—has rendered our social philosophy and social policies archaic and obsolete. There is good evidence to suggest that the United States suffers from an intellectual and policy lag in dealing with the problem of economic insecurity. We cling to an individualist conception of society and sentimental notions of rugged individualism. Our social policy, or lack thereof, fails to recognize that as our society has become more affluent, and therefore more specialized and interdependent, the individual's capacity to control his economic destiny through hard work and parsimony diminishes.[2] Empirical evidence attesting to the inadequacy of our present social security system is reasonably abundant. Relatively speaking, the United States' social security system is perhaps the least developed of any industrialized nation in the world. For example, each of the six Common Market nations spends a substantially larger percentage of its national income on

[2] Harry G. Johnson, *Money, Trade and Economic Growth* (London: George Allen and Unwin, Ltd., 1962), Chap. 9.

social security programs than does the United States.[3] It should be no surprise that a program-by-program appraisal of America's social security system recently led Cornell University's Andrew Hacker to the conclusion that the United States simply does not yet have a welfare state. As he sees it,

> Those who do not earn their own way are looked upon as second-class citizens who may be relegated to the subsistence level. Any claims they make for public support are not entirely legitimate and do not really carry the status of rights. Indeed we have such [welfare] programs not so much for political purposes . . . as for aesthetic reasons. The suspicion often arises that the rest of society pays them off at the lowest possible rate just so they won't be seen starving in the streets and hence upset public sensibilities.[4]

Ironically, a salient defect of our social security programs is that they frequently tend to be of least benefit to those who need economic assistance the most. Only about one-half of those families and individuals now classified as poor receive any transfer payments at all.[5] ". . . the fundamental paradox of the welfare state" as it exists in America is "that it is not built for the desperate, but for those who are already capable of helping themselves."[6] And the fact that decisions to expand the welfare state and therefore alleviate the consequences of economic insecurity lie in the hands of the relatively opulent majority who have not experienced economic insecurity does not suggest that in the foreseeable future we will have a social security system commensurate with the over-all wealth of our society.

Given my emphasis upon the distribution of the national income, as opposed to Dr. Walker's primary concern with expanding its size, it will come as no surprise that we differ on

[3] See Joint Economic Committee, *European Social Security Systems* (Washington: Government Printing Office, 1965), p. 11, and *Social Security Bulletin*, June 1965, pp. 28–32.

[4] Andrew Hacker, "Again the Issue of 'The Welfare State,'" *New York Times Magazine*, March 22, 1964, pp. 114–115.

[5] *Economic Report of the President, January 1964* (Washington: Government Printing Office, 1964), p. 68.

[6] Michael Harrington, *The Other America: Poverty in the United States* (Baltimore: Penguin Books, 1962), p. 172.

a number of more specific questions of policy. Let me mention briefly three of these.

1. I am much less willing than Dr. Walker to endorse an expansionary fiscal policy heavily committed to reducing taxes rather than to increasing government spending. Clearly many existing sources of economic insecurity reflect an arbitrary and unequal distribution of the costs of economic progress. These costs—of which structural unemployment may be a prime example—can best be alleviated, not by cutting taxes, but by increased government spending, in this instance on education and vocational training. The stimulation of aggregate demand through tax cuts is an oblique and uncertain way of resolving unemployment caused by serious market imbalances.[7] And in looking to the future, I see growing evidence to suggest that future sources of economic insecurity may lie increasingly outside of the private sector of the economy. Tax reductions will simply not give rise to the social goods and services requisite to mitigating the social and economic insecurity associated with water pollution, air pollution, urban blight, and inadequate law enforcement.

2. Even if for political reasons tax cutting must prevail as the major policy technique for achieving full employment, I would favor tax cuts of different types than those advocated by Dr. Walker. In evaluating Dr. Walker's tax proposals we must not lose sight of the fact that the effects of corporate and highly progressive individual income taxes upon incentives and investment are justifiably open to debate. Nor must we forget that a fundamental purpose of business taxation is to reduce investment and thereby permit noninflationary public expenditures. Furthermore, long-standing inequities in the tax structure favorable to businesses, e.g., the treatment of capital gains, depletion allowances, and the overly liberal interpretation of business expenses, make the corporate income tax more formidable on paper than in practice. In any event, if my premise

[7] See the statement by John Kenneth Galbraith in Joint Economic Committee, *Hearings on the January 1965 Economic Report of the President* (Washington: Government Printing Office, 1965), particularly pp. 13–15.

that economic insecurity is closely tied to the distribution of income is reasonably accurate, then the case for further cuts in corporate taxes and in rates applying to high-income recipients is thereby weakened.

3. Dr. Walker is of the opinion that to redistribute income toward greater equality "run[s] the risk of impairing the very efficiency which is one of the most desirable attributes of a market economy." Surely this traditional argument is due critical reappraisal. The least economically secure members of society who find themselves in a vicious circle of poverty can hardly be expected to possess the morale, the incentive, the training, or perhaps even the physical vigor to realize their potential contributions to the national output.[8] Furthermore, to the extent that our social policy fails to provide economic security, individuals and businesses will be motivated to adopt and promote efficiency-decreasing techniques and policies to achieve security. Are not featherbedding, price-fixing agreements, and demands for tariff protection frequently born of economic insecurity? There is certainly some reason to believe that an efficient social security system will foster, rather than conflict with, the goal of an efficient economic system.[9]

If we must make a choice between a rapidly growing but highly unequally distributed national income and a more modestly expanding but more equally distributed national income (and I am unconvinced that this is a necessary choice), it is not self-evident that the former choice is inherently superior. Although society must not allow economic efficiency to be undermined by humanitarian sentiments, neither can society tolerate economic efficiency untempered by humanitarianism. Perhaps the greatest attribute of the opulent society is its capacity to afford a modest amount of inefficiency in the interest of economic equity and security.

---

[8] A strong positive correlation exists between educational attainment and per capita production. See Frederick Harbison and Charles A. Myers, *Education, Manpower and Economic Growth* (New York: McGraw-Hill Book Co., 1964).

[9] See Johnson, *Money, Trade and Economic Growth*, pp. 194–195.

Comment by WALTER S. HENRION

There certainly can be no argument with the concept outlined in Dr. Walker's paper that the extent to which man's material wants are satisfied depends on the efficiency with which society combines its uses of human labor, natural resources, and capital goods, and I might add, in view of Dr. McConnell's comments, the distribution of the product or income of the system. In this quest for security, man's material wants may be regarded as his needs during both his productive and nonproductive years. As a general premise, there is probably little argument that ultimate economic security is to be achieved only when a society produces enough goods and services to meet the current needs of its people and, at the same time, accumulates sufficient savings to provide for the needs of their nonproductive years.

Nevertheless, it must be apparent that the most violent argument is raging around the world as to what type of economic organization can best combine and utilize those essential elements of production—human labor, natural resources, and capital goods. This debate is accompanied by ever shifting emphasis on free enterprise, government domination and direction, and the combination of these two fundamental forces. Dr. Walker's discussion of the major or fundamental characteristics of differing types of economic organizations seems to be directed primarily to some differences between the so-called "socialistic" and "capitalistic" systems. I direct your attention to what appears to be the dilution of the fundamental principles of both of these two widely divergent systems. In the Soviet Union, reliable current reports indicate that while state ownership is retained, monetary incentives to stimulate private initiative and achieve greater production are being infused into the Soviet economic system. Compensation related to achievement rather than need results in widely different standards of living but a higher *average* standard for all, another characteristic of the capitalistic system. While government continues to dominate the socialistic countries, an effort to gain the benefits of individual initiative could well lead to a resurgence of demands for greater individual economic and political liberty. And, in any event, as the production methods and results of socialistic mechanisms become discredited, the security of man throughout the world may be enhanced by the greater acceptance of the principles of incentive for, and initiative of, individuals and private organizations.

However, as Dr. Walker has indicated, Western governments are assuming an even greater role in the economic affairs of their societies. And there can be little argument that, in the relatively short span of some thirty years, these Western democracies have adopted many socialistic principles and programs. And there are many who believe that this trend which has blunted personal incentive and initiative is in the process of retarding the economic progress of our capitalistic market economy. Although socialism is adopting some of our free-enterprise principles, the achievements of the capitalistic system during the history of our country certainly raise questions about the advisability of our adoption and expansion of the principles of socialism. Let us be particularly wary of turning over to government the making of decisions which can be made so much better by the general public through the operation of a free-market economy.

After describing so well the major criteria for judging the performance of a market economy—efficiency, equity, capacity for growth, and stability—Dr. Walker has documented the convincing and successful performance of the United States market economy during the post-World War II period and especially during the 1960's. He has given major credit to both the fundamental characteristics of a market economy and federal economic policies. It seems significant to me that such federal policies represented some relative diminution of the government sector of the total economy. The tax credit for business investment in new equipment, the new IRS guidelines for depreciation, income tax cuts, and the reduction of excise taxes for both individuals and corporations all made significant contributions to a return of investment and consumption decision-making to those individuals and organizations in the private sector of the economy.

Dr. Walker's discussion of federal tax policies brilliantly points up how our present archaic tax picture weighs so heavily on our economy. At the same time, he cautions against the indiscriminate use of tax cuts which could lead to an unsustainable rate of economic growth, inflation, and a subsequent economic decline of substantial proportions. However, I suggest, and it is my purpose to introduce some controversy into this discussion in so doing, that income tax cuts for both individuals and corporations do not have to await slack in the economy in the form of unemployment and unused plant and equipment. If the additional demand created in the private sector of the economy by tax cuts is offset by a decline in demand or the rate of spending by the federal government, the economy might well experience an acceleration of the trend toward a more dominant private sector without the "overheating" and concomitant problems of inflation and subsequent decline of effective consumer demand. With the success of the most recent tax cuts, the projection of ever increasing tax revenues during the next few years, and remembering the transition from an economy dominated by government expenditures to a peacetime economy immediately following World War II, it might not take too much courage for some administration to push for more and more tax cuts even when the economy seems to be utilizing almost entirely its manpower and productive facilities. But it must be emphasized that at such a time, the increase in demand generated by these tax cuts would have to be offset by reductions in federal spending if we are to avoid the pitfalls pointed up by Dr. Walker.

In view of the vital role of these federal tax policies, Dr.

Walker performs a real service in reminding us that lags involved in moving the federal fiscal apparatus and unreliable economic forecasting make the results of tax cuts and compensatory federal budget policies highly unpredictable. In seeking to reduce the drag on our free-enterprise system now exerted by our present tax structure, the uncertainties of the future may well be underscored during this era of the optimistic "new economics."

There can be little argument that the difficulties of tailoring tax and fiscal policies to fit perfectly with emerging economic conditions point up the necessity of complementing such policies with a flexible monetary policy. Of course, there has been continuing controversy over monetary policy during the boom of the 1960's. However, examination of the sharply rising curve of the money supply throughout this period strongly suggests that monetary policy has had far more to do with ever increasing demand than have tax and fiscal policies. This record of ready availability of credit or money throughout most of this period has important implications. First of all, the availability of funds accompanied by rising short-term interest rates and essentially stable long-term rates has been unique. It has demonstrated at least some effectiveness of the Treasury and the Federal Reserve in their efforts to manage the capital markets so as to influence significantly both the domestic economy and our country's international balance of payments. Secondly, the Federal Reserve System apparently has been employing a new philosophy or technique during this expansionary period. It has been apparent that during most of this period the Federal Reserve has been following a policy of making funds readily available for further expansion as long as reasonably efficient workers and unused productive facilities are available and no definite evidence of price inflation is apparent. In general, the monetary policy of the Federal Reserve during this period has been more steadily expansive than in previous years. There is considerable evidence and a substantial body of opinion that, during the past twelve to eighteen months, monetary policy has been far too expansive, coupled with prevailing tax and fiscal policies, to be consistent with our objective of a stable economy growing at a sustainable rate. This expansive monetary and credit policy has accelerated the boom and now threatens the liquidity of the entire banking system. Record bank-credit expansion may have pushed the demand for consumer durable goods and the construction of plant and equipment to unsustainable levels. It is being argued that the expansive monetary policy during the boom has stripped the Federal Reserve of the tools and the flexibility to fight a future business recession.

However, the conscientious, dedicated, and independent efforts of the Board of Governors of the Federal Reserve under the continuing guidance of its present brilliant and forthright chairman, Mr. William McChesney Martin, holds forth substantial hope for the flexible monetary policy so strongly advocated by Dr. Walker in his paper. Unfortunately, the unreliability of economic forecasting which plagues effective tax and fiscal policy also afflicts flexible monetary policy. It is the unreliability of forecasting which concerns me most in this pursuit of economic stability.

The emphasis which Dr. Walker places on stability in unit labor costs as a major factor contributing to the stability and growth of the economy is most interesting to me. In view of the importance of this factor, employers, labor, and government should all cooperate in making certain that unit labor costs do not outrun the increase in the rate of productivity. It becomes increasingly apparent that this is the key to the avoidance of inflation, the reduction of unemployment, and the formation of capital. Although the wage-price guideposts established by the federal government have undoubtedly made some contribution to a "new climate of opinion," as claimed by the Council of Economic Advisers, they should not be regarded as being the key to economic success. In other words, some pat formula laid down by government decree does not assure the stability of unit labor costs. Unit labor costs will be determined by the terms of the contracts hammered out by business management and labor leaders at the bargaining table, and, of equal importance, by the cost of capital and the efficiency with which management puts it to work. Whether labor should receive all of the benefits of increased productivity is questionable. The investment of capital in more efficient and automated plants has been primarily responsible for the stability of unit labor costs. If such investment is to be continued at an adequate rate during the indefinite future, a fair and adequate return on such capital must be a reasonable prospect. Interference by government in this bargaining process can have most unfortunate effects upon capital investment and, hence, unit labor costs.

The relationship between cost-price stability and unemployment as outlined by Dr. Walker appears to have twofold significance in this quest for security. First of all, if more of our young people can be educated and trained before they enter the work force, they will be equipped to handle more productive jobs and, as a result, their own personal economic security will be enhanced. Secondly, the greater availability of more employable and competent workers will permit more expansive fiscal and monetary policies which will promote orderly growth of the economy on a sustainable basis. As Dr. Walker has indicated, this highly desirable kind of growth can be achieved only if these trained workers enter the labor force at wage levels and with capital equipment or tools which assure stable unit labor costs.

In his discussion of the so-called guideposts and guidelines which have been established by the Kennedy and Johnson administrations, Dr. Walker properly points up the dangers of these measures. They are "voluntary" only in name and strike at the roots of private initiative, self-interest, the profit motive, and the competitive pricing which provide the drive of the free-enterprise system. Despite the earlier-mentioned tax and fiscal policies which have regained something for the private sector of the economy, the so-called "voluntary" control of the flow of capital to foreign countries and the heavy-handed domination of the recent steel industry negotiations by the federal government raises the specter of business being further controlled by government decree. As Dr. Walker has indicated, a much better approach would be one which gives effect to the forces of a free-market economy. Hopefully, as a result of the favorable experience of recent years, all the segments of our society will realize that everybody benefits from the greater output of a more efficient and stable economy.

It is a cliché to say that economics is not an exact science. In fact, it is so inexact that the forecasts of economists are taken with a grain of salt by many thoughtful people. Nevertheless, the market economy so eloquently described and supported by Dr. Walker is the production marvel of world history. As such, it has made vast contributions to the economic security of man. The evidence submitted by Dr. Walker strongly suggests that this system is working even more effectively as its processes and forces become better understood. He holds forth the hope that its dynamic growth will continue with only minor interruptions.

The key to this achievement may well be regarded as the better understanding throughout our society of the economic principles and forces of our system. The results of this educational process may well be the most significant contribution of this era to man's quest for economic security.

A Military Scientist's View

GENERAL THOMAS S. POWER, USAF (Ret.)

Commander-in-Chief of the Strategic Air Command and Director of the Joint Strategic Target Planning Staff at the time of his retirement in 1964, GENERAL THOMAS S. POWER was an active military flyer for more than thirty-five years. During World War II, after service as a B-24 pilot with the 304th Bomb Wing in North Africa and Italy, he was transferred to the Pacific theatre, where he led the first large-scale fire bomb raid on Tokyo and held the post of Deputy Chief of Operations of the Strategic Air Forces during the atomic bomb attacks on Hiroshima and Nagasaki. In 1954, following six years as Vice Commander-in-Chief of the Strategic Air Command, General Power was appointed commander of the Air Research and Development Command, which at that time had been assigned the task of expediting the nation's ballistic missile effort. In April, 1957, he returned to SAC as Commander-in-Chief and was promoted to four-star rank.

In addition to many military decorations—among them the Distinguished Service Medal, the Silver Star, the Legion of Merit with one cluster, the Distinguished Flying Cross, and the French Croix de Guerre with palm—General Power has been accorded the high papal honor of investiture as a Knight of St. Sylvester with Grand Cross. In 1959 he received the Air Force Association's H. H. Arnold Award as "Aviation's Man of the Year," and in 1964 the National Conference of Christians and Jews presented him with its citation for his service to peace and the brotherhood of men. General Power is the author of *Design for Survival*, published in 1965.

My subject tonight is "Design for Survival in the Nuclear Age: or The Prevention of General Nuclear War Through the Maintenance of a Posture of Overwhelming Military Superiority." I will use the Strategic Air Command as a vehicle to develop this thinking. You will agree with me, I am sure, that this is a logical choice when you consider that if today this country should be subjected to a surprise nuclear attack, the Strategic Air Command is charged with delivering, with their bomb bays and their missiles, some 90 per cent of the striking power of the free world.

I will start with SAC's mission, which, realistically stated, is to be prepared to conduct strategic air operations on a global basis, so that in the event of sudden aggression it can mount simultaneous nuclear retaliatory attacks designed to destroy the war-making capacity of an aggressor to the point that he no longer has the will or the capacity to wage war. What is important here is, first, that the Strategic Air Command had and still has the capability to carry out this mission, and second—and even more important—that the Sino-Soviet bloc have been and still are aware of this capability. We believe that our strength and the Sino-Soviet awareness of it have acted as a potent deterrent to all-out nuclear war. Some may disagree, but I like to point to the record as clean: the world has *not* been engaged in an all-out nuclear war. And let me assure you that this is a good way to keep it, for if we should ever get into such a war there will be no winners, only losers in varying degrees. I can put it another way: if nations resort to the use of thermonuclear weapons to settle their differences of opinion or to accomplish their goals, then mankind will have reached its highest plateau of stupidity. I'm not saying that we won't reach that plateau—only that it is a worth-while goal not to arrive at it.

The reason we have not been in a nuclear war to date, the reason there is still a country known as the United States of America, is just this: we have not merely been as strong as the Sino-Soviet bloc, or a little bit stronger. We have had and still have such overwhelming military superiority that if any knowledgeable nation seriously considered engaging in a nuclear exchange with the United States, they would have to reject the idea because they would know that they would be destroyed, literally and figuratively. I can say this with some assurance because in addition to commanding SAC, in 1960 I formed an organization known as the Joint Strategic Target Planning Staff, which I operated until I retired. I wrote the war plans for the free world; I know what everybody is contributing; I had access to all the intelligence; and I know what the execution of our war plan will involve. So I know what I am talking about when I make the statement that no nation today would seriously consider engaging in a nuclear exchange with the United States because they realize that to do so would mean their literal and figurative destruction. Of course, there is only one country that has the capability to even consider such an exchange.

Our real mission, then, has been one of deterrence, of preventing a nuclear war through the maintenance of a posture of overwhelming military superiority. We have achieved this posture as a result of actions that were taken and decisions that were made some ten or fifteen years in the past. They include, for example, the decisions to build the hydrogen bomb; to build the B-47, the B-52, and the B-58 strategic bombers; and to build the Atlas, the Titan, the Minute Man, and the Polaris ballistic missiles. These are the decisions and actions that have given us our security.

The question now before the house is: Will we be able to maintain this superiority in the future? Is it technically feasible? Is it economically feasible? My answer is an absolute affirmative, provided—and this is a big proviso—that we want to. We have in this country people who are undoubtedly just as sincere as

I am in trying to prevent a nuclear war and in desiring to assure the future of a sovereign nation known as the United States of America, but who offer a different solution—a blueprint for general and complete disarmament. Now I submit to you that these two methods are incompatible; they are diametrically opposed. You can no more arm and disarm at the same time than you can dress and undress at the same time. A decision will be made as to which of these methods to follow. It will be the most important decision that is made in your lifetime, and I would like to think that it is influenced by an informed public. Not a public that necessarily understands all the complexities and the fine points of global strategic nuclear warfare, but one that does understand some of the basic principles involved. These are not complex; on the contrary, they are simple. And tonight I would like to discuss with you some of the basic principles behind our present successful formula of deterrence through strength as opposed to some of the other philosophies of deterrence, such as the minimum deterrent and the finite deterrent, that are bandied about today. I would like to expose the fallacies in these two philosophies and in the dream of disarmament.

Let me begin with our present successful formula of deterrence, preventing a war. Mind you, any fool can get into a war; it's the easiest thing in the world, particularly for a rich, fat, soft fool. It takes a hard, smart nation to stay out of war on honorable terms in today's world. There are three basic principles of deterrence that the public should understand. First, in order to deter, you must have a creditable military capability to achieve a military victory under any set of circumstances or conditions. You can't bluff; you have to have it. This takes us to the second, somewhat more sophisticated basic principle: you must not only be strong, you must let everybody know you are.

Publicizing our superiority is difficult in the United States for several reasons. One is that in the past everything connected with the military was clothed in secrecy, probably rightly so. Today, however, if you want to impress other nations with your strength, you have to let them know about it. But we have people in this country—very fine, altruistic people—who are so sensitive to world opinion that if we make a show of strength and someone, either friend or foe, calls us "capitalistic warmongers" or "saber rattlers" or "atomic maniacs," these people want to go hide in a corner. If you are sincere in trying to prevent a war, this is a dangerous pastime. You don't have to be particularly brilliant to figure it out. Look what happened not so long ago. We had a man named Hitler who wrote a book and told us what he was going to do. He made some probing tests to see how we would react, and you know what our reaction was to many of these tests: we did nothing. Mr. Neville Chamberlain, a well-meaning gentleman, went to Munich, came back, and said: "I have brought peace in our time." That peace lasted exactly eleven months.

Hitler did do one useful thing—he left tens of thousands of words, millions actually, documenting his plans, telling what influenced them, what caused him to change them. We have studied this documentation, and I can tell you what opinions he arrived at. I'll put it in blunt language: he had the impression that we—the free world—were weak, we were gutless, we were so afraid of war that we would give in to any demands rather than fight. He was wrong, but it took fifty million casualties to prove that he was wrong. History is full of such examples; they are as old as time. Yet today we have fools wandering around the country holding sit-ins and march-ins and teach-ins about Vietnam, and they are creating the wrong image. They are giving Ho Chi Minh the idea that we are weak, that we are afraid, that we will tire and get out of there; and it keeps him going. Of course, if he had any brains he would realize that he is in a hopeless situation, that he hasn't the strength to stand up to us, whereas we have the strength to wipe him off the face of the earth if we wanted to. So what keeps him going? Only one thing: he thinks we'll come apart at the seams. The people from whom he derives this impression think they are talking peace; but they are precisely the type of people who cause wars, because they encourage the gangsters, the Hitlers and the

Ho Chi Minhs, and they have to share with them some of the responsibility for causing wars. We have learned these lessons in our lifetime; we really shouldn't have to recite them again.

I have talked about the first two basic principles of deterrence —the necessities of possessing strength and of showing that you possess it. Now let me talk about the third one. Today you no longer deter with the size military force that you have in being, but with the size military force that you have left after you have been subjected to a surprise attack by bombers or missiles or both. In fact, to find the actual deterrent you must go one step further. You deter with the size military force that a potential aggressor *thinks* you will have left after he has subjected you to the surprise attack he is planning against you.

Today we are in the missile age. There are missile bases all around this city, and they are all over the Middle West. We have missiles by the hundreds; our potential enemies have them by the hundreds. They are accurate, they are reliable, they carry huge warheads. There is no operational defense in being against them in the world today. Man has never built, nor can he build, anything that will withstand a direct hit by a high-yield nuclear weapon. We looked into it at SAC headquarters some years ago. We were going to build what we call a DUCC, a Deep Underground Command Center. We had some of the finest engineering firms in the world study the problem, make the drillings and the borings, and they reported that if we went down some 4,400 feet, into pre-Cambrian rock, we possibly could build a structure that would withstand a direct hit if it had a fantastic G loading. *Possibly.* Let's consider this. If the missiles exist, are accurate and reliable, and carry big warheads, if there is no defense against them and nothing can be built that will withstand a direct hit by them, how can we feel confident that our deterrent force will survive and really be a deterrent force?

We use four basic strategies for weapons system survival, and I think it is necessary that the public be informed about them. The first, which applies only to manned bombers, is called "Fail-Safe Positive Control." This is the operation that

Burdick and Wheeler wrote a novel about.[1] It is a simple principle. You arrive at the maximum amount of warning you can be sure of. This is the warning we get of a ballistic missile attack from BMEWS—the Ballistic Missile Early Warning System, huge radars at Clear, Alaska, in Greenland, and at Fylingdales, England. These radars detect enemy missiles at about their apogee and warn the commander-in-chief of SAC and the commander of the Air Defense Command in Colorado Springs at the speed of light. They tell them from approximately where the missiles were fired, approximately where they are going to land, and—most important of all—in how many minutes. How long that will be depends on where your base is located: if it is in the northern part of the United States, you have some thirteen minutes; if it is in Florida, you have about nineteen minutes.

The idea here is to tailor as large a percentage as possible of your manned bomber fleet to be off the ground and on its way in less time than the warning allows. The Strategic Air Command has for years maintained some 50 per cent of its bomber fleet in this state of readiness. It is tested daily; it is a proven system. The commander-in-chief of SAC has the authority to launch this force. He has to have this authority to ensure the survival of the fleet. There is no time to call people up or hold conferences. You have to move and move right now. The bombers are loaded with weapons, they are targeted, and—so far as the crews are concerned—they are going to war. But they fly out only to a predesignated geographical position, remaining a predesignated period of time; then if they have not received the "go" code, they fail-safe and return home. The "go" code can be issued only by the President of the United States; that is the law of the land. In no sense is such a maneuver provocative. The bombers do not fly near enemy

---

[1] An allusion to *Fail-Safe*, a 1962 novel by Eugene Burdick and Harvey Wheeler, which erroneously assumed the possibility of a mechanical failure in the system with the result that an enemy target was accidentally bombed. See Sidney Hook, *The* Fail-Safe *Fallacy* (New York: Stein & Day, 1963).—*Editor's Note*

radars or enemy borders, and no one in the country except the people at SAC knows the fleet has been launched unless he has been told.

This system was started in October, 1957, when I had the Stategic Air Command. People were concerned about it. As I said, this book *Fail-Safe* was written. After that we had many, many experts visit the Strategic Air Command; as the commander, I was impressed that we had such a number of experts in the United States. They came out in great droves, and they looked this system over critically, trying to find a flaw in it. They went away satisfied that it is a safe system; let me assure you that if somebody puts an ashtray in a computer in the SAC underground there is no chance of our bombing Moscow. To sum up: this first method, Fail-Safe Positive Control, will ensure the survival of the SAC manned bombers.

We use a second strategy called *dispersion*, that is, we disperse the forces. When I commanded SAC we had bombers spread around some hundred bases; I understand a few have since been closed down. So that one Soviet missile could not destroy two of our missiles, our missiles are located miles apart. This is a good strategy; however, it is not all-encompassing. But it does make the Soviet planner's job more difficult. We couple it with another strategy called *hardening* that applies to our missiles. The Minute Man missile silos of massive concrete and steel are hardened to some five hundred pounds to the square inch. They will withstand a near-miss, but not a direct hit, for, as I told you before, there is nothing in the world that will withstand a direct hit by a hydrogen bomb. But our Minute Man system does impose three things on the Soviet Union: accuracy of their missiles; simultaneity—because these Minute Men dispersed all over the middle western part of the United States are loaded and aimed and can all be fired thirty-two seconds after a valid order is received at the launch-control facility. Thus the Soviet planner must plan to strike every one at the same time, a very difficult tactical task and one which imposes the third requirement—numbers.

Before looking at how this strategy works, let me make a

rather trite statement. If you are planning to start a major nuclear war, make sure that you will be around when it is over. Make sure that you have a high confidence factor in your plan to destroy the nuclear retaliatory systems in the country you are attacking. This is a basic principle for all planners. Let's assume that I am the Soviet planner, writing a war plan for my boss—a war plan which, if he executes it, will have a high confidence factor that he will survive. This means that I will have to plan to destroy every one of these Minute Man silos. Let's begin with Minute Man silo number one, near Cheyenne, Wyoming. To arrive at the number of missiles that must be fired against this silo to give a high confidence factor, I multiply three factors—the accuracy of my missiles, their reliability, and the warhead yield. Assuming some values—not necessarily accurate values, but neither are they wild guesses—we'll say that my missiles have an 80 per cent reliability factor; in other words, if we fire one hundred missiles, eighty of them will reach the target area. We'll assume that they have a two-nautical-mile Circular Error Probable for accuracy, and that each missile warhead carries the equivalent of seven million tons of TNT. If I multiply these factors together, I come up with the number twenty. This is the number of missiles I must plan to fire against silo number one in Cheyenne in order to have a 95 per cent confidence factor that it will be destroyed. So you see that hardening is good strategy; it forces the attacker into numbers and makes them less sure that they can knock out our retaliatory forces. A word of caution, however. As the accuracy improves—and that is the current trend—the number of missiles required to ensure a high confidence factor decreases dramatically, to about two.

I have spoken of three strategies: positive control applying only to our bombers, dispersion of both bombers and missiles, and hardening. The fourth strategy is called *mobility*. It is based on the simple principle that you keep the weapons system moving on a random pattern twenty-four hours a day. It applies to the Polaris submarine and the airborne alert. It is the best principle of all for the survival of the weapons system, since with the system moving at all times, the Soviet planner has a zero confidence that he will know where it will be on D-Day and H-Hour of the attack he is planning. It is because we use all four of these strategies that I can stand here tonight and state with some confidence that if anyone in the world should launch a surprise nuclear attack against the United States, a sufficient percentage of our retaliatory forces would survive and deliver their weapons, with the end result that the nation launching the surprise attack would be destroyed. The fact that this is general knowledge has stabilized many aspects of the world situation.

The question now is: Will we maintain the proper system in the future? Speaking for myself, I don't know. There are two other deterrent postures that I think the public should have some conception of. One is called the minimum deterrent; the second —and more dangerous—is called the finite deterrent.

The fallacy of the minimum deterrent is easily seen. Its proponents say that we have too much weaponry—that we have a tremendous stockpile that would enable us to blow the world up two or three times over, the so-called overkill. But the people who write books and articles claiming that it is pointless to pile up weapons, that we would just be blowing things up time after time, have failed to understand one vitally important fact: there is a big difference between a weapon in your stockpile and a delivered weapon. The problem is not building weapons but applying them. How much damage was done to the Japanese Empire with the warships at Pearl Harbor or the airplanes at Hickam Field on December 7, 1941? None; they were destroyed before they got into action. We call it DBL—destroyed before launch. This is the big problem of the minimum deterrent. There is also the problem of attrition. Since the enemy doesn't like you to retaliate, they try to stop you, and you lose some of your bombs. You also have mechanical failures and human errors. In other words, not every bomb you build ends up on an enemy city or an enemy target, only a certain percentage, if you're lucky.

Another illogical bit of reasoning by the people who argue for the minimum deterrent is based on the assumption that they know a nation will be deterred if a certain number of targets are destroyed. But whoever makes such a statement has to base it on what he knows, on his own background and experience—and in this instance it is Americans talking. In this connection, let's look at the figures for loss of life in the great American catastrophes: the Chicago fire, the San Francisco earthquake, the Galveston flood, the Civil War, World War I, and World War II. In the fire I believe we lost 250 people; in the earthquake, 350; at Galveston, 5,000; in the Civil War some 500,000, including a great number who died of disease; some 200,000 in World War I; and 300,000 in World War II. In contrast, look at the Soviet Union or the Sino-Soviet bloc that we are trying to deter. In the typhus epidemic after World War I, Russia lost some 5,000,000 people; 5,000,000 starved to death in the great famine of the 1920's; another 5,000,000 lost their lives while Stalin was trying to dispossess the landowners; and in World War II supposedly some 20,000,000 were lost. As for China, her Minister of Defense allegedly made the statement: "We are the only nation in the world that can lose half our population and still be bigger than any other country." He is talking about losing 350,000,000 people. We cannot possibly say what the minimum deterrent would be in the case of these two countries because no one knows, not even the rulers of the Sino-Soviet bloc themselves. Although a certain loss of life and certain economic losses might deter them today, six months from now they might change their minds—they might be willing to absorb more punishment. I'd put the minimum deterrent as an extremely dangerous policy to follow.

You—by which I mean the people of the free world—could go to the other extreme. If you wanted to devote the efforts of every man, woman, and child toward building a military, you could undoubtedly build a military machine so powerful that even an idiot would know that he would be destroyed if he attacked the free world. We don't recommend this course, because you would inevitably destroy politically and economically what you are trying to protect militarily. But somewhere in between these two extremes there is a sensible margin. The problem is how to arrive at it.

Now let's consider the other philosophy, the finite deterrent. This actually was conceived in the services, and it is more palatable and more salable—and more dangerous. According to this line of thought, all you need for deterrence is a few missiles that you are sure will survive and have the assured capability to destroy X number of cities and a certain percentage of the enemy's economy. There are two weak points here. One, again its proponents assume that the enemy will give up after the destruction of a certain number of cities. They forget that the people in the cities have nothing to say about what happens. These wars are started and waged by the dictators, the gangsters running the countries. Thus, although the people might object to the destruction of more cities, it is quite possible that the ruler, in a deep underground shelter, would take a different view. The second and more important fallacy is that this philosophy ignores the enemy military. You do not have a military force of your own that is designed to destroy the enemy military; it is left intact, and it can come and kill you. Here let me interject that when I was writing the war plans, my number one moral responsibility was to save American lives and the lives of our allies from the enemy military; killing the enemy came second. But the finite deterrent is built around the concept of killing the enemy; it completely ignores the protection of people in this country and attacks only the enemy military that happens to be co-located in the target cities.

I would like to say a bit more about the so-called overkill, because so many people, particularly now that I am out of uniform, say to me: "Why are you always talking about maintaining overwhelming superiority? You know we've got more weapons than we need—we have enough to blow up the whole world." Perhaps one way to explain overkill is to make war planners of you. Let's say that we're going to write a hypothetical war plan together. Our target is a Soviet ICBM in Russia—an Intercontinental Ballistic Missile targeted at the

United States, its aiming point Lincoln, Nebraska. The object of our war plan is to destroy that target. As war planners, we have to write a plan to destroy all the targets. So let's pick a weapon out of our arsenal and choose a weapons system. We have many different types of weapons, many different weapons systems. But say, just for example, that we pick a bomb that is now sitting down in Fort Worth, Texas, in a B-52. According to basic principle number one, all we have to do is get one bomb there—one bomb will destroy any target in our war plan. Unlike the situation in World War II, when we had to deliver thousands of bombs and go back again and again, today one bomb successfully delivered will do the job. Now that we've selected the bomb, we pick a bomber that is on the alert; if it isn't on the alert, we're wasting our time, because it has a very small mathematical chance of surviving. But it is on the alert, so it has about a 95 per cent confidence factor of surviving. Now we will downgrade it for mechanical failure. We have records of literally hundreds and hundreds of thousands of flights that can tell us what percentage of mechanical failure can be expected out of so many hours of flight. Drawing on this experience, we downgrade our bomber 3 or 4 per cent. In order to get to its target, it will have to refuel. Here again we draw on past experience—we have refueled millions of times; we used to refuel somewhere in the world every three or four minutes, twenty-four hours a day. We downgrade our bomber 3 or 4 per cent for missed refueling due to weather or mechanical failure. Now the next phase: we enter enemy territory and they are going to try to shoot us down. We'll take the bomber through the actual known enemy territory against the actual known defenses. We'll give the enemy credit for being very proficient in their defense and downgrade our own performance accordingly, thus arriving at an attrition factor. As we approach the bomb release line, the bombardier has to find his target. It may be raining, it may be night; still he has to locate it. Here again from our hundreds and hundreds of thousands of training flights we know our mathematical chance of finding that target and delivering the weapon. Now the bomb is released. There is a mathematical chance of failure for the weapon itself—that it may be a dud—and this has to be applied. Now let's add up all the attrition factors and say that we arrive at a 50 per cent chance of its getting there and destroying our target. This is what we put in our war plan.

If you are satisfied, you people in Lincoln, with being 50 per cent confident—satisfied with a 50 per cent chance to live if we get in a war—we can let it go at one bomb. But if you'd rather feel a little surer, let's send another bomb. But if we send two, we are 75 per cent, not 100 per cent, confident—that is mathematical law. There is still a 25 per cent chance that we'll miss the target and that enemy ICBM will come over here and kill you. So we send three, four—now we're getting up close to 90 per cent; five, six—not all of the same type, and we'll send them from different weapons systems, to arrive at a confidence figure that is satisfactory. But it is impossible ever to reach 100 per cent. As we start getting up to six, seven, and eight, each additional weapon buys very little. However, I assure you that when I was writing the war plans on what we call Time Sensitive Targets—targets that can kill Americans—we had at least a 90 per cent confidence factor that those targets would be destroyed regardless of how a war started. Even so, there is still a 10 per cent chance that you'll miss them. Now perhaps you see how it is that the people who have never seen a war plan, have never heard a gun go off, can say: "But you're sending six weapons against that target and it only takes one to destroy it, so you're destroying it six times over." They overlook the fact that there is a 10 per cent chance you'll miss it completely. The point is, if you are wise and intend to be around for a while, it is much better to plan ahead and put the odds in your favor.

I'd like to speak now for a few minutes about disarmament, because, of course, this is what I am arguing against. I am trying to build the case for what we have been doing, even though I'm aware this is a very unpopular cause. You are looking at the lone military man in the United States who unequivocally opposed the test ban treaty, who testified against it before the United States Senate. Why did I do that? Being against the test ban treaty in this country is almost like being against motherhood and in favor of sin. The preamble of the test ban treaty states that its goal is general and complete disarmament, and—if any of you should be in doubt—I do not believe in general and complete disarmament. It is a strategy, I am told, that goes back to about 455 B.C. The Nationalist Chinese ambassador to Washington told me that there were a couple of warring factions in China at that time; their war had been dragging on for a long time, and neither side had been able to secure an advantage. Then one had a brilliant idea: why didn't they disarm? But once he had conned the other man into disarming, the strength ratio changed, and he jumped on his foe, let him have it, and that ended the war.

A good lawyer can, from the study of history, indict disarmament as a major cause of war. We have seen its consequences in our lifetime; we've had the Kellogg-Briand Pact, the Five-Power Naval Treaty, and the Treaty of Versailles, which forbade Germany to rearm. In that connection there's a story about an incident in Germany during the mid-1930's, when Hitler was secretly rearming. A poor German worker had a job in a baby carriage factory. When his wife became pregnant, he got the bright idea of smuggling out the various parts for a baby carriage and then reassembling them in their basement. When the baby came, they'd be all set with a baby carriage. He smuggled the parts out, and every evening he'd go down to the basement and work on the reassembling job. It got close to the baby's time, and the wife asked the husband: "How are you coming along with the baby carriage?" He scratched his head and answered: "You know, I can't understand it. Every time I put that darn thing together I come up with a machine gun." Hitler built up his forces right under our eyes, and so did the Japanese. I spent two years in the Philippines, from 1936 to 1938, and it was perfectly apparent that we were going to have a war. In those days it was difficult to hide what you were doing; it took time to build conventional weapons. Today the situation is different. It is difficult to expose modern weapons and keep them exposed.

All that I have been saying bears on the problem of inspection. One of the basic premises when we took the missiles out of Cuba—or at least Krushchev took them out—was that there would be on-site inspection. As you know, we have never had it. And what concerns me is that the public will be so anxious for disarmament that they'll start giving in on the requirement for on-site inspection. In fact, even with inspectors on-site it might still be possible to hide modern nuclear strategic weapons.

In considering disarmament, it's a question of whether the people concerned are sincere—it can't work unless all parties sincerely want to disarm. If you accept that as a premise, let's look at the logic of the requirement for disarmament. Assuming that the nations sincerely mean they will never resort to the use of armed force to accomplish their goals, then what difference does it make whether they are armed or disarmed? They won't ever use their weapons—if they are sincere. But if one nation is on the level and the other is not, the stage is set for the classic takeover. It has happened time after time in history, and I'd say we're ripe for it again. The trouble is that the people who argue for disarmament are fine and good and full of altruism—they want to save the world, just as Mr. Chamberlain wanted to save the world. He was a good man, but you can be hurt by your friends as well as by your enemies.

However, let's say that we are convinced that we should try this noble experiment; we decide that we will disarm. In that case, I have a suggestion. Let's try it at home first. Let's try it in these United States—disarm the policemen in Washington, D.C., in New York City, Chicago, and Los Angeles. Let's see if we can live together as human beings in our own domestic society without beating one another's brains out, without murder, rape, and robbery. Then, and only then, in my judgment, could you cautiously approach the world of international gangsters and see whether or not you want to try and live without armed forces to protect you.

I no longer make the mistake of underestimating the appeal of the disarmament concept. Five or six years ago I thought it was a dream; I could not believe that it would ever make headway. But the disarmament idea is a very salable product, and its progress has amazed me. In Geneva in 1961 the United States offered a blueprint for general and complete disarmament. We have a State Department policy paper, called 7277, concerning general and complete disarmament in a peaceful world, and there are three steps for obtaining it. This proposal has tremendous backing. What I'm saying, on the other hand, is extremely unpopular. Nonetheless, if we want to assure the survival of this country in this world today, we must maintain our strength. The best friends you have, the only real friends, are those nuclear weapons. They are the only ones that won't let you down, the only ones you can depend on. If you do away with them, you will not have a nation. In fact, if the Strategic Air Command hadn't been around for the last fifteen years, there would not today be a nation known as the United States of America. You would not be here.

I can sum up all my hopes and aspirations for the future survival of our sovereign nation in just three brief phrases: keep America strong; exploit space for military purposes; and get another manned bomber in SAC to replace the B-52.